DATE DUE

FE 14 '05			
DE 27 '04			

Greece

Greece

BY ANN HEINRICHS

Enchantment of the World
Second Series

Children's Press®

A Division of Scholastic Inc.

NEW YORK TORONTO LONDON AUCKLAND SYDNEY
MEXICO CITY NEW DELHI HONG KONG
DANBURY, CONNECTICUT

Frontispiece: Hillside town of Thira on Santorini Island

Consultant: Dr. Amy J. Johnson, Assistant Professor of History, Berry College,
Mount Berry, Georgia

Please note: All statistics are as up-to-date as possible at the time of publication.

Book production by Herman Adler Design

Library of Congress Cataloging-in-Publication Data

Heinrichs, Ann
    Greece / by Ann Heinrichs
        p. cm. — (Enchantment of the world. Second series)
    Includes bibliographical references and index.
    ISBN 0-516-22271-6
    1. Greece – Juvenile literature. [1. Greece] I. Title. II. Series.
DF717 .H38 2002
949.5—dc21   2001047722

Greece

Contents

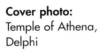

Cover photo:
Temple of Athena,
Delphi

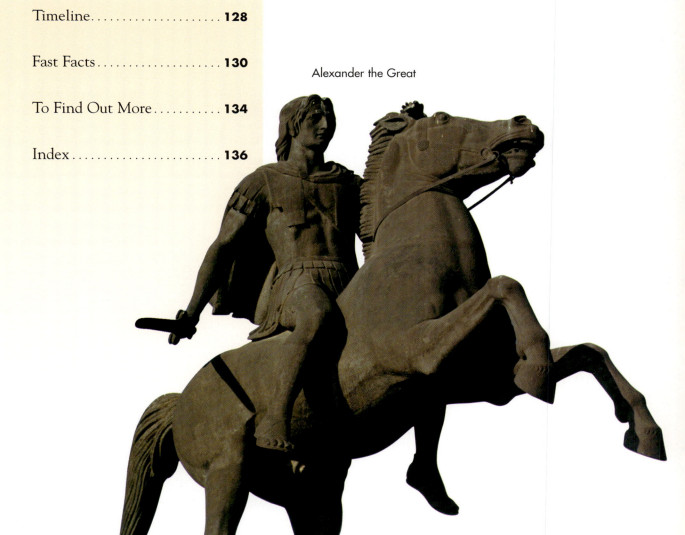

Meteora Monastery

Alexander the Great

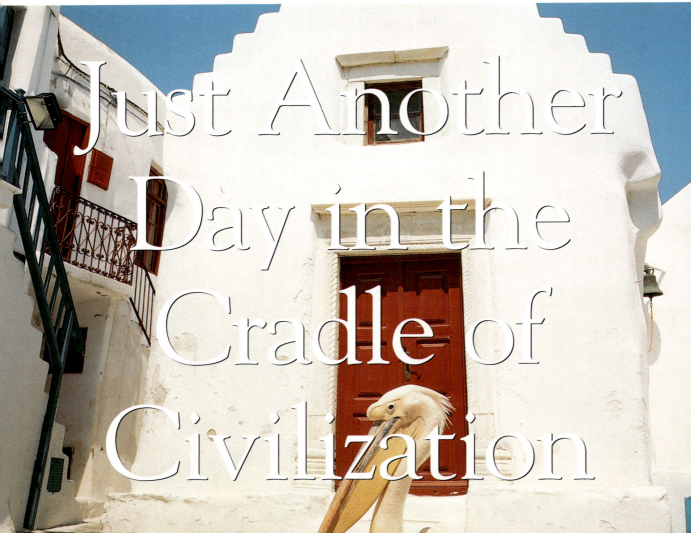

Just Another Day in the Cradle of Civilization

DANGLING HIS LEGS OVER THE SEAWALL, NIKI TOSSES A fish to Petros the pelican. It's not the real Petros—the mascot of Mykonos for more than thirty years. He was killed in a traffic accident before Niki was born. This is a younger pelican, but everyone calls him Petros just the same.

It's still early morning, but Niki's father is closing up his business for the day. If it were summer, his little vegetable stand by the harbor would be sold out by now. Tourists and café cooks would have snatched up every last leafy scrap. It's only February though—still the winter season on Greece's Mykonos Island.

Niki and his father pack up their leftovers, load them onto the donkey, and head up the rocky hillside toward their home high above the town. As they enter their whitewashed court-yard, Niki smells delicious aromas drifting from the kitchen. Tonight it's their turn to hold the weekly pig roast. Winter may be slow for business, but for villagers on Mykonos, winter traditions are very much alive. Every week a different family roasts a pig and invites the neighbors in to make sausages and feast on the succulent pork.

With the rest of the day before him, Niki wanders into the hills, where wild hares are nibbling grass among the prickly pears and gray-green stones. From his favorite perch, he gazes across the rocky hills of Mykonos. Those rocks, they say, are the bodies of giants that Hercules killed. Niki knows it's only

Opposite: **A pelican is the mascot for the island of Mykonos.**

Just Another Day in the Cradle of Civilization **9**

A church built among the rocky hills of Mykonos

A fisherman mends his nets.

a myth, but as his eyes follow the outline of the rocks, he's sure he can see gigantic shoulders, noses, and chins.

Beyond the giants, Niki can see the island of Delos, where the great men of Athens paid homage to Apollo. Niki himself has seen the colossal marble lions that stand guard over Apollo's sacred lake.

Down at the waterfront, Petros waddles among the fishermen mending their bright yellow nets. Pirates used to hide out in secluded coves along the coast. Hercules may be a fantasy, but Niki knows that the pirates were real. The townspeople of Mykonos built their narrow, winding alleyways just to trick the pirates so they'd get lost in the maze.

GREECE

● Cities of more than 40,000 people
○ Smaller cities and towns

0   100 miles
0   150 kilometers

Selected Archaeological Sites
1. Akrotiri (on Santorini)
2. Delphi (Mt. Parnassus)
3. Epidaurus
4. Knossos
5. Mycenae
6. Olympia
7. Troy

Geopolitical map of Greece

BULGARIA

FYROM

ALBANIA

Struma R.
Vardar R.
Néstos R.
Évros R.

Kilkis
Pella
Serrai
Kavala
Xanthi
Thessaloniki
Alexandroupolis
Kastoria
Thasos
Samothrace
Gulf of Strimón

Meteora Monasteries
Alliákmon R.
Mt. Olympus
Gulf of Salonika

TURKEY

Corfu
Corfu
Paxos
Ioánnina
Pinios R.
Larissa
Kardhitsa
Volos

Limnos

NORTHERN SPORADES

IONIAN ISLANDS

Leukas

Lesbos

Missolonghi
Euboea
Skyros
Khalkis

AEGEAN SEA

Chios

Ithaca
Cephallonia
Patras
Navariti
Corinth
G. of Corinth
Andros

Zakynthos
Gulf of Kiparissia
Alfiós R.
Nauplion
Sparta
★ Athens
Piraeus
Saronic Gulf
Tinos
Mykonos

Samos

IONIAN SEA

Kalamata
Eurotas R.
Gulf of Messini
Gulf of Laconia
Gulf of Argolis
Mirtóön Sea
Paros
Naxos

Patmos
Kalymnos

CYCLADES ISLANDS

Kos

Kythera
Milos
Santorini

Sea of Crete

Chania

Rhodes
Rhodes

Karpathos

DODECANESE ISLANDS

Crete
Herakleion

Greece

N
W   E
S

MEDITERRANEAN SEA

Children dress in costumes during carnival season.

Niki can hardly wait to relive those days when carnival season begins next week. Other kids may be dressed as Batman or Zorro, but Niki will be a pirate. For three whole weekends, he and his friends get to wear their carnival costumes and zigzag through the town, ducking into hidden corners, jumping out at revelers and pelting them with eggs, and squirting each other with foam from spray cans. But for now, there's a pig roasting on the spit, and it's time to scramble home.

Niki's life on Mykonos is the Greece most outsiders never know. For centuries, however, people around the world have shared his sense of wonder at the history, culture, and traditions of Greece.

Greece is a small country. In fact, it would fit inside the state of Alabama, with room to spare. However, Greek traditions—both real and pretend—still kindle our imaginations and shape our world today.

Greek mythology gave us awesome superheroes, such as Hercules, Jason, and the Titans, as well as terrifying villains, such as the Cyclops and the Minotaur. Ancient Greeks also gave us models for art, science, sports, logical thinking, government, and democracy itself. This is why Greece is called the birthplace of Western civilization.

Aside from its glorious past, Greece is a bright, sunny vacation spot. The skies are brilliantly clear, and gentle breezes drift in from the sea. Greece's sparkling beaches and deep blue waters help make it the most visited country in Europe.

Greece's beautiful beaches attract many tourists.

Some travelers come to enjoy the sunny weather, the scenic countryside, or the simple pace of life. Others come to stand in awe before the ruins of ancient worlds. Either way, no one leaves without memories to last a lifetime.

Mountains, Islands, and Wild Things

An old Greek legend explains how Greece came to be. When God created the world, it says, he sifted all the soil onto the earth through a strainer. After every country had enough good soil, he tossed the stones left in the strainer over his shoulder—and there was Greece!

Opposite: **Greece is a country of many islands.**

Geographical Features

Area: 50,942 square miles (131,940 sq km)

Highest Elevation: Mount Olympus, 9,570 feet (2,917 m)

Lowest Elevation: Sea level along the Mediterranean Sea

Number of Islands: More than 2,000; 170 populated

Largest Island: Crete, 3,189 square miles (8,260 sq km)

Average Annual Precipitation: 51 inches (128 cm) in Corfu; 16 inches (40 cm) in Athens

Length of Coastline: 9,333 miles (15,020 km)

Navigable Rivers: None

Greatest Distance, North-South: 350 miles (587 km)

Greatest Distance, East-West: 345 miles (555 km)

Viewed from the air, Greece does seem to be a jumble of stones dumped into the sea. It's a rocky, mountainous country, with gulfs and bays cutting deeply into its jagged coast. Thousands of islands lie off the coast. They are the tips of mountains rising up from the ocean floor.

Greece juts out into the Mediterranean Sea at the tip of Europe's Balkan Peninsula. By land, it borders Albania, Bulgaria, and the Former Yugoslav Republic of Macedonia (FYROM) to the north. To the east is Turkey. But most of Greece is encircled by water. Two arms of the Mediterranean Sea surround it—the Ionian Sea on the west and the Aegean Sea on the east. No point in Greece is more than 85 miles (137 kilometers) from water.

Greece was once a mass of rock that lay completely undersea. It sat at the edge of a tectonic plate—a shifting section of the earth's crust. When that plate smashed into the rest of Europe, the collision created high mountain ranges. That plate is still moving, causing earthquakes all around the Aegean.

Mountains and hills cover more than three-fourths of Greece. The Pindus Range runs down the mainland like a spine, from northwest to southeast, dividing the country in two. In the north, the Rhodope Mountains separate Greece from Bulgaria.

The Pindus Range divide Greece in two.

Looking at Greece's Cities

Thessaloniki (above), also called Salonica, is Greece's second-largest city and port. It was named after the sister of Alexander the Great. The city is a blend of new and old, with luxury boutiques and Byzantine churches along its tree-lined streets. At the waterfront is the Platia Aristotelous, an open square looking out on the sea. In the northern heights is the old city, with many historic churches.

Piraeus is the port city of Athens and the third-largest city in Greece. Besides its shipping and fishing industries, Piraeus is an engineering and chemicals center. Its Hellenic Maritime Museum features more than 2,000 exhibits covering twenty-five centuries of sailing history.

Patras is Greece's fourth-largest city and the major port of the Peloponnese. The main part of town lies between the harbor on the west and the old acropolis in the east. Shady parks and squares are scattered around the city. Near the harbor is the church of Ayios Andreas (St. Andrew). It houses the skull of St. Andrew, who was martyred in Patras in 70 A.D.

Herakleion is the capital and commercial center of Crete (shown below is Port of Iraklio in Herakleion). It's named for the mythological hero Hercules, who saved Crete from a raging bull by seizing its horns. (From this legend we get the saying "taking the bull by the horns," which means taking command or taking control.) Herakleion was the port for the ancient Minoan city of Knossos—now a major archaeological site. Favorite gathering spots in the modern city are Liberty Square and Venizelos Square, with their shops and outdoor cafés.

The city of Rhodes is the capital of the island of Rhodes. The Colossus of Rhodes, a gigantic statue whose legs straddled the harbor, was one of the Seven Wonders of the Ancient World. (That's where we get the word "colossal," meaning huge.) An earthquake destroyed the 98-foot (30-m) statue in 226 B.C. Now two bronze deer statues guard the harbor. The medieval Knights of St. John were headquartered in Rhodes, and its old town preserves their castle and fortress. Along cobblestoned Knights' Street are the inns where knights from seven nations lived.

Thrace's countryside
is perfect for farming.
In the background is a
mosque and its minaret.

Northern Greece

Thrace is the far-northeastern region of Greece. It shares a border with Turkey, and many Thracians are Turkish-speaking Muslims. Rising across the countryside are minarets, the towers of Muslim mosques. Tobacco, grains, and cotton grow on Thrace's hills and plains.

Philip's Philippi

Philippi is an archaeological site in Macedonia. It's named for King Philip II of Macedonia (382–336 B.C.), who took the city in 356 B.C., fortified the town, and named it after himself. Over the next twenty years,

Philip conquered all of Greece. He was preparing a Greek army to make war on the Persian Empire when one of his bodyguards killed him. His son, Alexander the Great, carried on after him.

Macedonia, west of Thrace, is Greece's largest region and its richest farming district. Its broad plains produce wheat, corn, cotton, tobacco, and rice. Thessaloniki is the capital of Macedonia province and Greece's second-largest city. On the Chalcidice Peninsula is Mount Athos, Greece's most famous group of monasteries.

Epirus, the northwest region of Greece, lies just across the Pindus Range from Macedonia. The Ionian Sea washes Epirus's western shores, and just to the north is Albania. Epirus is mountainous, and not many people live there. Sheep graze on the mountainsides, however, and their wool is important to Epirus's economy.

Monasteries built high on Mount Athos

Central Greece

Thessaly is a fertile plain in central Greece encircled all around by high peaks. One is Mount Olympus, Greece's highest peak. On top of Olympus, according to Greek mythology, lived the twelve Olympian gods. Wheat and cotton are Thessaly's most important crops. Larissa and the seaport of Volos are the major cities.

The Pinios River cuts Thessaly in two. Before it reaches the sea, the Pinios courses through a deep, luxurious gorge called the Vale of Tempe. Its narrowest point is a dark, mysterious stretch known as the Wolf's Jaws.

Below left: **Mount Olympus, Greece's tallest peak**

Below right: **The Vale of Tempe**

The region south of Thessaly is the heart of Greece. On the Attica Peninsula is Athens. It was the center of ancient Greek culture, and now it's the nation's capital. Farther west is Mount Parnassus. It's the site of ancient Delphi, home of the famous oracle of Delphi.

Southern Greece

Southern Greece is the Peloponnese Peninsula, or Peloponnesus. It's not really a peninsula any more. The narrow isthmus of Corinth used to connect it to the mainland. Now the Corinth Canal cuts through the isthmus.

Regions		
1 Attica	6 Central Greece	11 Eastern Macedonia/Thrace
2 Crete	7 Western Greece	12 Peloponnesus
3 Southern Aegean	8 Ionian Islands	13 Thessaly
4 Northern Aegean	9 Central Macedonia	
5 Epirus	10 Western Macedonia	

The Peloponnese is shaped like a hand with four fingers that reach to the southeast. Many of Greece's most famous archaeological sites are on the Peloponnese. Ancient ruins stand in Corinth, Mycenae, Epidaurus, Sparta, and Olympia. In the center of the Peloponnese are the mountains and high plains of the Arcadia region. Mountains extend out from Arcadia into each of the peninsula's "fingers."

Pine forests and tough shrubs cover most of the Peloponnese, but crops grow well on the fertile coastal plains.

White water in the Vouraikos Gorge

On the northern edge of the peninsula, the major cities are Corinth and Patras. East of Patras is the breathtaking Vouraikos Gorge.

The Islands

Islands make up about one-fifth of Greece's land area. By some counts, there are more than 2,000 Greek islands, but people live on only about 170 of them. The main island groups are the Ionian, the Cyclades, and the Dodecanese.

The Ionian Islands lie west of the mainland in the Ionian Sea. With Italy just across the sea to the west, Ionians have been heavily influenced by Italian culture. Italian-style architecture can still be seen on the islands, and many of Greece's Roman Catholics live there. There are seven main islands, and Corfu is the largest and most populated. Ithaca is famous as the home of the mythical hero Ulysses in Homer's epic poem the *Odyssey*.

One of the seven main islands in the Ionian Island group.

Homes built into the hillside in the Cyclades

Another island group, the Cyclades, dots the Aegean Sea off Greece's southeast coast. Like most Aegean islands, they are rocky and arid. Their neat, white-washed houses, set high on the hillsides, are dazzling in the sunlight. The name Cyclades comes from *kyklos*, the Greek word for "circle." The Cyclades form a ring around Delos, which was sacred to ancient Greeks as the birthplace of the god Apollo.

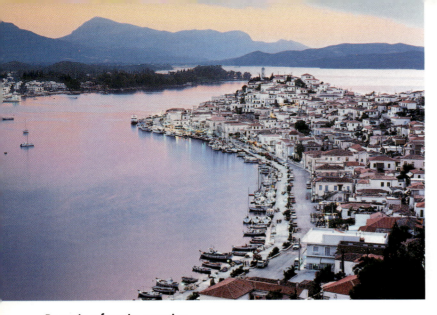

Paros is a favorite vacation destination.

Today the Cyclades are popular holiday spots—especially Santorini, Mykonos, Paros, and Naxos. Santorini is actually the rim of an ancient volcano. An eruption blew the top off, leaving only the crater's edges. Some people believe Santorini is the site of the legendary continent of Atlantis. Excavations have turned up a fabulous ancient city called Akrotiri, adding more fuel to the legend.

The Dodecanese Islands lie far across the Aegean, along the coast of Turkey. Their name means "twelve," and there are a dozen major islands in this group. Rhodes, off the southwest tip of Turkey, is the largest. It's nicknamed the "island of roses," but its flashy red flowers are really hibiscus.

Poppies, as well as hibiscus, cover rocky hillsides.

Scattered to the north of the Dodecanese are the islands of Samos, Chios, Lesbos, Lemnos, Samothrace, and Thasos. Across the Aegean, the large island of Euboea hugs the mainland coast. Nearby are the islands of Skyros, Skiathos, Skopelos, and Alonissos.

Long, narrow Crete, at the southern edge of the Aegean, is in a class by itself. It's the largest of all the Greek islands and the fifth-largest island in the Mediterranean Sea. Crete's most famous ancient site is Knossos—the center of the Minoan civilization and home of the mythical beast the Minotaur.

The "bull's horn" of the Palace of Knossos

Three Thousand Hours of Sunshine

Greece is sunny and bright. Its skies are often brilliantly clear, and cool breezes blow in from the sea. Greece enjoys more than 250 days of sunshine every year. If you figure that there are twelve hours of sunlight a day, that comes out to 3,000 sunny hours a year!

Like its seaside neighbors, Greece has a Mediterranean climate. In other words, summers are hot and dry, and winters are mild and wet. December, January, and February are the coldest months. Greece warms up fast in spring, and temperatures are highest in July and August.

It's much cooler in the mountains of Greece than along the coasts. Snowfall in the mountains creates perfect ski conditions for winter holidays. Crete's highest peaks keep their snowy caps almost all year 'round. Northwestern Greece is the wettest region, and the southeast is the driest. Rain, when it comes, is often a quick downpour that clears up just as quickly. The sunshine never stays away very long.

Forests, Blossoms, and Shrubs

In ancient times, almost all of Greece was covered with forests. Over the centuries, trees were cleared for shipbuilding and farming. Nibbling goats took their toll on the foliage, too. Now only about one-fifth of the country is forested. Maples,

Pine trees grow along rocky cliffs in Greece.

Rows of olive trees in the Peloponnese

chestnuts, beeches, pines, and Grecian firs cover the mountainsides. Northern Greece is the most heavily wooded area.

A sharp, tangy smell in the air is a sign that eucalyptus trees are nearby. Rows of aromatic eucalyptuses turn country roads into cool, shady lanes. Plane trees and pepper trees also provide roadside shade. Aleppo pines are a common sight on the rocky coastal slopes. Their trunks are twisted, and their bark is gray.

Greeks have cultivated olives since ancient times. Olive trees, with their gnarly trunks and silvery leaves, live almost everywhere except in the mountains. They don't grow very tall, but they live a long time. Some olive trees planted in the thirteenth century are still yielding olives!

The Gift of Athena

According to Greek mythology, an argument broke out between Athena, goddess of wisdom, and Poseidon, god of the sea. Both thought they should be the guardian of Athens. They finally agreed that whoever gave the city the best gift would win. Poseidon struck the earth, and the gift of water gushed forth. Athena kicked the ground, and up sprang an olive tree. The other gods declared Athena the winner, for her gift was more valuable.

About half of Greece is covered by plants called *maquis*. These are low trees and shrubs with shiny, leathery leaves. One example of maquis is gorse, with its brilliant yellow flowers. In the dry southeast are cactus, agave, and other succulents—plants that can store water to survive.

Above: **These spiny plants are typical of the tough vegetation that flourishes in Greece's dry, rocky soil.**

Right: **Prickly pears grow in the dry southeastern region of Greece.**

The National Garden

Ducks, swans, and peacocks mingle with visitors at the National Garden in Athens. This peaceful, green park has more than 500 kinds of trees, shrubs, and flowers. Broad avenues wind through the flowerbeds, leading past statues, pavilions, lakes, and ponds. Tucked away amid the foliage are cafés and even a zoo. The National Garden used to be the Royal Park—the palace garden of the royal family. In 1923, it was renamed the National Garden and opened to the public.

In springtime, the meadows and hillsides are ablaze with wildflowers. Wild orchids, hibiscus, rhododendrons, bougainvillea, and hardy rock roses flourish. Irises, crocuses, and tulips grow high in the mountains in the cool shade of firs and pines, while bright scarlet poppies sprout on the rockiest

A field abloom with wildflowers

Valley of the Butterflies

Every summer, hundreds of thousands of butterflies fill the shady valley of Petaloudes in northwest Rhodes. (*Petaloudes* is Greek for "butterflies.") Actually, they're not butterflies but Jersey tiger moths. They fly in from all over Europe, attracted by the vanilla-scented resin of the valley's storax trees.

Wolves can still be found in Greece.

hillsides. In the countryside, the summer air is sweet with the aroma of wild rosemary, sage, oregano, and thyme.

Creatures in the Wild

Lions are a familiar image in ancient Greek art. This suggests that they may once have lived in Greece. However, as the forests have dwindled, so have the wild animals that lived there. Deer, wild boars, wildcats, and even some bears and wolves still lurk in the northern Pindus Range. Foxes and badgers are more common. They creep through the forests and scrublands looking for prey such as mice, hares, and squirrels.

Wild sheep and goats can be seen sometimes on the rocky hillsides. One very old species of goat lives on the island of Crete. It's the wild bezoar goat, an early form of the modern domestic goat.

Magpies, house sparrows, and blackbirds are common in Greece. Warblers and bee-eaters flit through the wooded hills, while partridges and quail scratch for insects on the forest floor. Along the coasts are sea swallows, gulls, and herons.

A bee-eater perches on a branch.

Golden Jackals

Golden jackals prowl across the hills and plains of the Peloponnese. At breeding time, they dig a hole in the ground to make a den. Newborn cubs stay in the den for about three weeks before venturing out into the world. Farmers and shepherds used to hunt jackals to stop them from preying on their chickens and lambs. In the 1980s, however, jackals were named a protected species.

Pelicans stop for a dip in the wetlands of Greece.

Thousands of birds pass through Greece on their migrations, and the country's wetlands make it a popular stopping place. The Evros and Nestos Rivers of Thrace widen into marshy deltas as they reach the sea. As many as 100,000 birds from northern Europe and Asia spend their winters there. These deltas are now wetland reserves.

Many of Greece's sea creatures end up on dinner tables. They include mullet, mackerel, bass, sardines, and tuna. Octopuses, squid, shellfish, and lobsters also live off the coast. Out in the open waters, boaters sometimes catch a glimpse of dolphins leaping up in graceful arches. The sea provides sustenance, but it also presents some danger to people. Swimmers have to watch out not only for sharks and moray eels, but also for sea urchins and jellyfish.

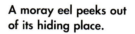

A moray eel peeks out of its hiding place.

The Glories of Ancient Greece

MUCH OF WHAT WE KNOW ABOUT ANCIENT GREECE has been dug out of the ground. Archaeologists have unearthed entire kingdoms that lay buried for thousands of years. Ancient Greeks left written records of their achievements, too. Beyond these sources, we have enchanting tales of gods and heroes to enrich our vision of the past.

People have lived in what is now Greece for at least 10,000 years. By about 3000 B.C., three civilizations were flourishing around the Aegean Sea. On the Greek mainland was the Hellenic civilization. Its name comes from *Hellas*, the Greek word for Greece. In the Cyclades Islands was the Cycladic civilization. Its people made white marble statuettes noted for their graceful, elongated style.

The third and greatest of the Aegean cultures was the Minoan civilization on the island of Crete. It is named for its legendary monarch, King Minos. According to mythology, King Minos fed young men and women to the dreaded Minotaur, a monster with a man's body and a bull's head. By about 2000 B.C., Minoan kings had luxurious palaces, and bustling cities surrounded their royal courts.

Opposite: **Bronze statue from late Hellenistic Greece**

Ruins of the royal apartments in the Palace of Minos

Meanwhile, new people were migrating into the mainland from the north. They set up farming villages and introduced the gods that would become the basis of Greek religion. These new people are called the Mycenaeans, after the fortified city of Mycenae in the Peloponnese. Among the buildings they left behind in Mycenae are domed "beehive tombs" and an acropolis with its stone Lion's Gate.

Beehive tomb at Mycenae

Legends from this time tell about King Agamemnon, the Trojan War, and Jason and the Argonauts. Centuries later, the Greek poet Homer used these tales to write his epic poems the *Iliad* and the *Odyssey*.

Mycenae fell around 1200 B.C. Then people called the Dorians invaded. They were warriors and had little interest in art or culture.

Local cults grew up around the gods and goddesses of Greek religion. Mount Olympus was the home of the twelve main gods, but there were many others. Long before Mycenaean times, Olympia and Delphi had been centers for the worship of Gaea, the Earth Mother. By the ninth century B.C., Olympia had become the sanctuary of Zeus, king of the gods. Delphi was dedicated to the god Apollo. He was believed to reveal oracles, or prophecies, through his priestess there. People would travel hundreds of miles to consult the Delphic Oracle before making big decisions.

Epidaurus was the sanctuary of Asclepius, the god of medicine. The sick brought offerings there in hopes of being healed. Asclepius's staff, with a magic serpent coiled around it, is the symbol of the medical profession today.

The Oracle of Delphi in a trance

The Twelve Olympian Gods

Greek Name	Roman Name	Responsibility or Significance
Zeus	Jupiter	king of the gods
Hera	Juno	goddess of marriage; wife of Zeus
Aphrodite	Venus	goddess of love and beauty
Artemis	Diana	goddess of the hunt and the moon; sister of Apollo
Hermes	Mercury	messenger of the gods; son of Zeus
Poseidon	Neptune	god of the sea
Apollo	Apollo	god of poetry, prophecy, medicine, and light
Demeter	Ceres	goddess of grain, agriculture, and harvests
Hephaestus	Vulcan	god of metalworking and fire
Athena	Minerva	goddess of wisdom; guardian of Athens
Ares	Mars	god of war; son of Zeus and Hera
Hestia	Vesta	protector of the home and family

(Dionysus [Bacchus], god of wine and revelry, is sometimes listed instead of Hestia.)

The Agora (main square) of Athens at the height of its glory

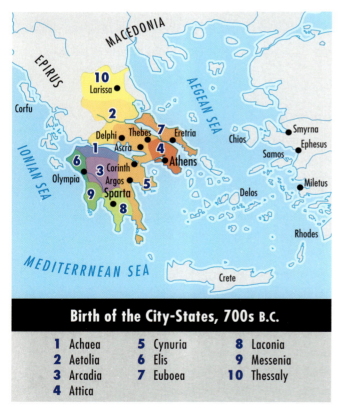

Birth of the City-States, 700s B.C.

1	Achaea	5	Cynuria	8	Laconia
2	Aetolia	6	Elis	9	Messenia
3	Arcadia	7	Euboea	10	Thessaly
4	Attica				

The City-States and Colonies

In the 700s B.C., the Greeks began to band together and form city-states. Each city-state had its own leaders, warriors, and economic system. They fought one another, too, and the city-state of Sparta grew powerful in the Peloponnese. Meanwhile, the city-state of Athens to the north was making its fortune on the sea trade.

One reason the city-states fought was that the mainland was getting crowded. People began to sail off and start new communities all around the Mediterranean. From about 770 to 550 B.C., Greek colonies sprang up in Asia Minor (present-day Turkey),

The First Olympic Games

Olympia was the site of the world's first Olympic Games in 776 B.C. At first, they featured only one event—the footrace—and the first champion was a cook named Coroebus. Athletes gathered to compete again every four years. Events were added for chariot racing, wrestling, boxing, long jumping, and javelin and discus throwing. To the victors went only one prize—a crown made of a wild olive tree branch. A strict code of honor prevailed at the Games. Anyone who broke it was expelled, fined, or even flogged.

All of Greece observed a "sacred truce" during the games. Warring peoples would lay down their arms in honor of Zeus and try to find ways to make peace. Olympic years were also used to mark time. For instance, people would say an event took place "in the third year of the tenth Olympiad."

The Games were held continually for almost 1,200 years. In A.D. 393, Theodosius, the Christian emperor of the Roman Empire, issued a decree against "pagan" practices. Since the games were dedicated to Zeus, that was the end of the ancient Olympics.

Syria, and the islands. To the west, Greeks colonized lands as far away as Italy, Spain, France, and North Africa. Meanwhile, Greeks began holding athletic contests at Olympia. The first Olympic Games took place in 776 B.C.

Around the same time, the poet Homer was collecting heroic tales that people had been passing down for hundreds of years. He turned the stories into lengthy epic poems. The *Iliad* tells the story of Achilles, Agamemnon, and the Trojan War. The *Odyssey* tells of the valiant hero Odysseus and his treacherous journey home from the Trojan War. Though laced with fantastic mythological details, Homer's epics contain a surprising number of historical facts.

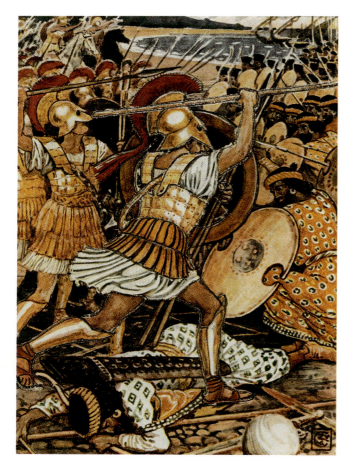

Athenians defeat the Persian army at the Battle of Marathon.

The Persian Wars

When the Persians invaded Greece, the city-states were forced to work together. In the first Persian War, which erupted in 490 B.C., Athens defeated a Persian force more than twice its size on the plain of Marathon. Athens and Sparta together drove off the Persians again in 481 B.C. The next year, in the battle of Salamis, an Athenian fleet of warships struck a deadly blow to the Persian fleet. One final battle, in 479 B.C., put an end to the Persian threat.

After the Persian Wars, Athens and Sparta returned to their own power struggle against one another. Athens gathered several city-states together to form the Delian League in 477 B.C.

The First Marathon

Legend has it that, when the Persians landed at Marathon, an Athenian runner named Pheidippides was sent to Sparta to ask for help. He ran the 156 miles (251 km) in one day and then ran back to the battle. After the Greeks' victory, he ran to Athens (26 miles/42 km) with the news. "Rejoice! We conquer!" he shouted—and then dropped dead from exhaustion. Modern marathon races are named in honor of Pheidippides's feat, although runners go for shorter distances than Pheidippides did!

With the Aegean islands and the Asia Minor colonies in its league, Athens was king of the sea. Its navy had no equal.

Sparta created a rival alliance called the Peloponnesian League. Its army became the strongest land-based fighting force in Greece. Soon Sparta's entire society revolved around building a strong military. Newborns who were judged to be weak were killed. Boys trained for the military from age seven to twenty and then served in the army until they were sixty. For all Spartans, life was disciplined and simple. There was no room for luxuries or leisure activities. This lifestyle gave us the word "spartan," meaning simple, self-disciplined, and lacking in comforts.

Classical Period: The Golden Age

The birth of Athens's Delian League marks the beginning of Greece's Classical Period, or Golden Age. It was a time of prosperity when art, culture, and democracy flowered. Athens became the major political power and cultural center of the Greek world. The glories of the Golden Age are mainly the work of a wise statesman named Pericles. He ruled Athens for thirty-two years—from 461 to 429 B.C.

The glories of the Golden Age can be attributed to Pericles.

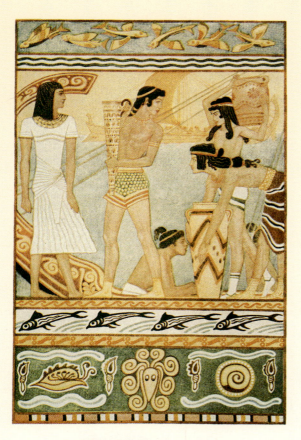

they spent a lot of time discussing politics. They met with friends in the *agora*, or public marketplace, and enjoyed parties called *symposia* (Greek for "drinking together").

Weaving and sewing were important women's tasks. Women wore their hair in ponytails or in braids arranged on top of their head. Athenian women could not wander around on their own. They could only leave their homes to attend religious ceremonies. In Sparta, however, women were free to move about. Both men and women wore simple tunics of linen or wool, adding a woolen cloak in cold weather.

All but the poorest homes kept slaves. Slaves were captives from wars, abandoned children, or children of slaves. They cooked, cleaned, carried water, guarded homes, and worked in fields, factories, and mines. It's estimated that slaves made up between 40 and 80 percent of ancient Greece's population.

Scenes from Daily Life

Children in ancient Greece used animal bones for dice. They also played with yo-yos, terracotta dolls, and clay animals with pull-strings. In school, boys studied mathematics, memorized Homer's poetry, learned to play the lyre (a harp-like instrument), and trained at athletics. Girls learned to read and write at home. They helped their mothers or worked in the fields—except in Sparta. Spartan girls learned wrestling, gymnastics, and combat skills. Spartan boys were taken from their parents at age seven for military training.

Men worked at trades, farmed, hunted, or went to sea. Athens granted voting rights to all free adult men in 508 B.C. Since men took part in the government,

Pericles made sweeping reforms. He strengthened the Delian League and made it easier for members of the lower classes to hold public office. Because he loved the arts and sciences, he encouraged thought and creativity.

One of Pericles's greatest achievements was rebuilding the Acropolis. This sacred city on a hilltop in Athens had been destroyed during the Persian Wars. Pericles hired an architect and sculptor named Phidias to oversee the project.

With a team of artists, architects, and craftsmen, Phidias designed a complex of dozens of sacred temples and sanctuaries. The most fabulous was the Parthenon, the main temple of Athena. Phidias created dramatic scenes in stone to decorate

The Parthenon, the main temple of Athena

Who Will Lose Their Marbles?

The Elgin Marbles are marble sculptures removed from the Acropolis 200 years ago. (Greeks prefer to call them the Parthenon Marbles.) Thomas Bruce, seventh Earl of Elgin, took the marbles in the early 1800s. He was Great Britain's ambassador to the Ottoman Empire, Greece's ruler at the time.

The largest piece of marble is from the Parthenon. It consists of fifty-six panels of a frieze—a long procession scene carved around the sides of the building. Other pieces came from the nearby Erectheion Temple—a column and a caryatid, or female statue that served as a column.

The Elgin Marbles are now housed in London's British Museum. They are at the center of a long-standing dispute between Britain and Greece. The British government believes that it acquired them fairly through its purchase from Lord Elgin, while the Greeks claim that the purchase was illegal.

Peloponnesian War, 431–404 B.C.

- Athens and its allies
- Sparta and its allies
- ★ Major battles

the outside of the temple. Inside, he sculpted a 40-foot (12-m) statue of Athena out of gold and ivory.

While Athens flowered, Sparta was plotting revenge. For years Athens had been harassing Sparta's allies, and finally Sparta declared war. This conflict, known as the Peloponnesian War, lasted from 431 to 404 B.C. Once the Persians joined the war on Sparta's side, Athens's defeat seemed certain. Finally, with their food supplies cut off, the Athenians surrendered. The Golden Age was over.

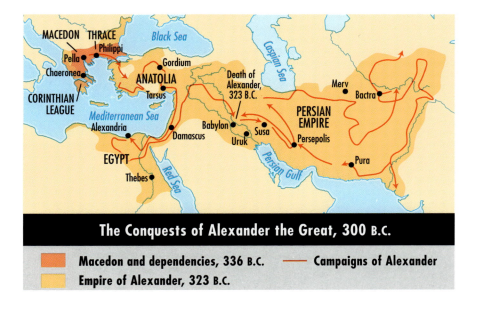

The Conquests of Alexander the Great, 300 B.C.

Macedon and dependencies, 336 B.C. — Campaigns of Alexander
Empire of Alexander, 323 B.C.

Philip and Alexander

The wars had weakened all of Greece. Thousands of able-bodied men were dead, the poor had grown poorer, and old disciplines had broken down. It was the perfect opportunity

Alexander the Great

Alexander (356–323 B.C.), son of Philip II of Macedonia, studied under the Greek philosopher Aristotle. As a boy, he trained his trusty black stallion, Bucephalus, who carried him into all the great battles of his life.

When his father died in 336 B.C., Alexander took command of the Macedonian and Greek army. With 35,000 men, he set out to conquer Persia. He defeated the Persian king Darius at the Battle of Issus (333 B.C.). Then he turned his sights to Egypt, conquered it, and founded the city of Alexandria in 332 B.C. Next he took Babylon, invaded eastern Persia, and continued into present-day Afghanistan and India.

By the age of thirty, Alexander ruled the world—that is, all of the world known to Greeks at the time. According to a famous legend, "When Alexander saw the breadth of his domain, he wept, for there were no more worlds to conquer." He died of a fever at age thirty-three.

for a takeover. In Macedonia, north of the Greek city-states, King Philip II saw his chance and took it. In 338 B.C., he conquered the Greeks in the Battle of Chaeronea. Philip's brilliant son Alexander was still a teenager then, but he commanded a wing of Philip's army.

Philip organized the Greek city-states into the League of Corinth. Greek soldiers were ready to follow him into Persia when he was murdered. Alexander succeeded his father and, with his well-trained army, conquered the vast Persian Empire and much more. In only ten years, Alexander's empire stretched from the borders of China in the east to Egypt in the west.

The Hellenistic Era

After Alexander died, his generals divided his empire among themselves. This period is called the Hellenistic Era. It was a time when Greek art, culture, and science spread throughout the empire. Greek artists and scholars were welcomed in prosperous cities from Antioch in Asia Minor to Alexandria in Egypt.

Meanwhile, to the west, the Roman Empire was engaged in conquests of its own. Macedonia and Greece, so close to Roman lands, were natural targets. After war broke out in 215 B.C., Rome soon got the upper hand.

Romans gradually took control over Greek regions until they destroyed the ancient city of Corinth in 146 B.C. This was the final blow in Rome's conquest of Greece. Now Greece became just another province of the Roman Empire.

Great Minds of Ancient Greece

Archimedes (287?–212 B.C.) invented all kinds of things, such as war machines for catapulting objects, and a "screw" for raising water out of a river. He's famous for springing out of a bathtub and shouting "*Eureka!*" ("I have found it!"). In the tub, he had figured out how to calculate the weight of an object that's floating in water.

Hippocrates (460?–370? B.C.) was the first doctor to use scientific methods to find what causes illnesses. All doctors today take the Hippocratic Oath, named after Hippocrates, in which they swear to practice medicine honorably and to do no harm.

The philosopher Socrates (470–399 B.C.) taught his students by asking questions that made them think. His most famous student was Plato (427–347 B.C.). Plato taught that appearances can't be trusted because they are constantly changing. The only way to reach the truth, he said, was to find the ideal concept that lies behind what we see.

Aristotle (384–322 B.C.) was a student of Plato. He focused on natural sciences, logic, ethics, and many other areas. His method of arriving at sensible conclusions is called Aristotelian logic.

Pythagoras (570–496 B.C.) (below) came up with a way to calculate the hypotenuse (longest side) of a right triangle—$a^2 + b^2 = c^2$. It's still called the Pythagorean theorem. But it was Euclid (365–300 B.C.) who developed most of what we study in geometry today.

Becoming a Nation

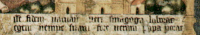

Under the Roman Empire, Greeks had no real power. They were free to pursue their usual trades—as long as Rome reaped most of the profits. The Romans admired the high culture they found among the Greeks. They adopted many of Greece's arts, customs, and religious practices as their own. Soon the entire Roman Empire took on Greek ways. Greek gods and goddesses were given Roman names, although their roles stayed the same. In time, the new religion of Christianity would take the place of the gods as the empire's official faith.

Neither Christianity nor Judaism was welcome in the Roman Empire because these religions challenged the authority of the emperors. Christianity was growing quickly in the first two centuries A.D., and Christians were executed by the thousands. That persecution ended when the emperor Constantine embraced the new religion.

The Byzantine Era

In A.D. 330, Constantine moved the capital of the Roman Empire from Rome to Byzantium. This marks the beginning of the Byzantine Era. Byzantium was an ancient Greek colony on a peninsula in Asia Minor. From a warfare point of view, it was a great location because it overlooked military frontiers on both land and sea. It was also an important trade center. The city was eventually renamed Constantinople.

Constantine had allowed freedom of religion. But when Theodosius became emperor in 379, he made Christianity the official religion of the Roman Empire. He banned all pagan cults and all remnants of ancient Greek religion. That included the Olympic Games.

When Theodosius died in 395, the Roman Empire split into eastern and western halves. After years of attacks by Germanic tribes, the Western empire fell in 476. The Eastern empire carried on as the Byzantine Empire, with Constantinople as its capital and Greek as its official language.

The emperor Justinian (527–565) did wonders for the empire. He fought off invaders, reformed the laws, and built new cites and public works. His grandest building project was Constantinople's Hagia Sophia cathedral.

Although Justinian defended his lands, the borders of the Byzantine Empire were never safe during his reign. Goths, Vandals, and Huns occupied much of Greece in the fifth century. Slavs stormed down from the north and held most of Greece for two centuries. One after another, Arabs, Bulgarians, Normans, Franks, Venetians, and Turks hammered

Hagia Sophia Cathedral

away at the empire. Nevertheless, Greeks carried on with daily life. Thessaloniki, Thebes, and Corinth became thriving industrial centers. Monasteries were built throughout the empire, many adorned with lavish artwork.

Relations between Eastern and Western Christianity were often tense. The patriarch of Constantinople led the Eastern Church, while the pope in Rome headed Western Christianity. In 1054, the two broke apart once and for all (see Chapter 8) in what is called the Great Schism (meaning "split"). They continued as the Roman Catholic Church in the West and the Greek Orthodox Church in the East.

Meanwhile, Muslim armies had taken over Jerusalem. In 1096, Pope Urban II launched the Crusades to win back the Holy Land from Muslim "infidels." Many Crusaders were poor, unarmed peasants who hoped at least to win spiritual rewards. Others joined in hopes of making a fortune. So it was with the Venetians. They joined the Fourth Crusade in 1204 and changed its target to Constantinople. They sacked the city and pillaged the churches, including the magnificent Hagia Sophia.

The conquerors divided the empire among themselves and installed Western bishops to rule over the Orthodox Church. In time, the empire became too divided and weak to withstand its biggest threat.

The Ottoman Era

Turkish warriors in Asia Minor, united as the Ottoman Empire, were gradually taking over Byzantine lands. By the late 1300s, the Ottomans occupied much of the Balkan Peninsula, including large parts of Greece. The final blow came in 1453, when the Ottomans seized Constantinople. After more than 1,100 years of power, the Byzantine Empire collapsed. In Greece itself, Athens fell in 1456. The feisty Peloponnese held out against the Ottomans until 1460.

The Muslim Ottomans allowed the Greek Orthodox Church to carry on. This helped Greeks to keep alive their sense of national identity. Greek was the language of the

The Renaissance

After the Ottoman conquest, many Greek intellectuals fled to Western Europe. A large community settled in Italy. They arrived with perfect timing, for Italians were just beginning to rediscover the classical era of ancient Greece and Rome. The Italians saw this period as an enlightened time. In contrast, they thought of the next thousand years as the Dark Ages.

This new awakening was called the Renaissance, which means "rebirth." Classical Greek and Roman art, sculpture, architecture, and literature became models for the Renaissance. The exiles had brought ancient Greek writings with them, and they helped nourish the blossoming movement. Renaissance ideals quickly spread throughout Europe. This marked the end of Europe's Middle Ages and the beginning of modern times.

Church, and religious festivals were an important part of Greek culture.

The Ottomans trained promising young Greek men for their army and for government jobs. In doing so, they created a class of privileged Greeks. Another elite group was the Greek sea merchants. The economy prospered as they traded west through the Mediterranean and east to ports on the Black Sea.

At the other extreme were ordinary peasants. As taxes grew more burdensome, they began staging revolts. Peasant bandits called *Klephts* lurked in mountain passes to attack and rob Ottoman officials. Many popular ballads glorified their bravery and heroic resistance.

The War of Independence

By the late 1700s, Greek merchants made up a well-to-do middle class. To improve Greek schools, they sent teachers to study in Western European universities. The Greek visitors to this region were surprised to find that Europeans looked on ancient Greek culture with reverence and awe. Once they returned home, they spread their newfound pride in their Greek heritage.

Patriotic Greeks began to form secret societies to work for independence from the Ottomans. One society was led by Count Alexandros Ypsilantis. With his encouragement, Greeks staged a major revolt. Fierce Greek fighters stormed down from the northern mountains into the Peloponnese in 1821. They battered one Ottoman stronghold after another, setting up local governments as they went along. This began the Greek war of independence.

The Valiant Bouboulina

Bouboulina, born Lascarina Pinotzis (1771–1825), was a famous heroine of the Greek war for independence. After losing two husbands to sea pirates, she bought the warship *Agamemnon*, headed out to sea, and led a squadron against the Turks. She took part in sea battles in 1821 and 1824, committing acts of piracy herself, and joined the Greeks' blockade of Nauplion. In 1825 Bouboulina was shot and killed during a family quarrel.

The Battle of Navarino broke the Ottoman grip on Greece.

Foreigners Step In

Many European artists, writers, and intellectuals were caught up in the passion and romance of the Greek independence movement. When the war began, they donated generously to the cause. They were known as the Philhellenes ("Lovers of Greece"). Even the British poet George Gordon, Lord Byron, went to Greece to fight. He sailed to the city of Missolonghi, which was suffering under a long Ottoman siege. Byron led a brigade of fighters and died of a fever there in 1824.

The Ottomans eventually won Missolonghi and went on to take Athens's Acropolis. Joined by allies from Egypt, Ottoman forces began ravaging the Peloponnese. Outraged at the slaughter, Great Britain, France, and Russia banded together with Greece. They demolished the Ottoman-Egyptian fleet in the sea battle of Navarino in 1827. This was the last great naval battle among ships under sail during the Greek war of independence. It proved a heavy blow to the Ottomans' weakening grip. In 1829, the last Ottoman troops withdrew. After 1,500 years of foreign domination, Greece was independent at last!

Independent Greece

With their capital at Nauplion, Greeks elected Ioannis Kapodistrias as their first prime minister, but he was assassinated within a couple of years. Great Britain, France, and Russia—called the "Great Powers"—had pledged to oversee and protect the new country until it got on its feet. In 1833, they installed a king—a seventeen-year-old Bavarian prince named Otto. Otto was an absolute monarch and ultimately led Greece into financial ruin. In 1844, Greeks forced him to make the country a constitutional monarchy.

George I came to the throne in 1864. A prince of Denmark, he had been chosen king by the Great Powers. Greece's National Assembly made sure King George had even less power than Otto.

Meanwhile, Greece was trying to restore its ancient lands. At independence in 1829, the country was only about half of its present-day size. Greece acquired the Ionian Islands from Great Britain in 1864. Then in 1881, the Great Powers persuaded the Ottomans to return Thessaly to Greece.

The island of Crete remained self-governing until it finally joined Greece in 1913. After the Balkan Wars with the Ottomans (1912–1913), Greece won back most of Macedonia and Epirus, and some of the Aegean islands. These moves were the work of the Cretan statesman Eleftherios Venizelos. This popular leader became prime minister in 1910 and made sweeping reforms to Greece's economy. He also persuaded Greece to join the Allied Forces in World War I (1914–1918), fighting Germany and its allies. After the war, Greece acquired Thrace and more Aegean islands.

Most of these changes took place while King George I was still on the throne. His fifty-year reign ended when he was assassinated in 1913. Then his son became King Constantine I. Since Constantine's brother-in-law was the kaiser (king) of Germany, Constantine wanted Greece to stay out of World War I. Many Greeks, however, wanted to enter the war. As a result of this conflict, he was forced to give

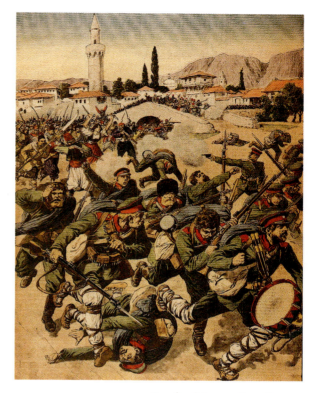

Greeks drive out invaders during the Balkan Wars.

Heinrich Schliemann

Heinrich Schliemann (1822–1890) was a German archaeologist who began excavating prehistoric Greece. As a child, Heinrich was fascinated with his history book's picture of Troy in flames. He always remembered this picture and believed that Troy was real, not just a legend in Homer's *Iliad*. When he grew up, he amassed a fortune in the grocery trade. Then he began to pursue his obsession—unearthing ancient Greece.

In 1868, near the Turkish coast, he dug up what he believed was the ancient city of Troy. Then he excavated Mycenae, which he believed to be King Agamemnon's royal city. In Mycenae's royal tombs, he discovered gold face masks, breast plates, and jewelry. This caused quite a stir, and archaeologists from Greece, Germany, and Great Britain continued his explorations.

the throne to his son Alexander I. After Alexander died in 1920, Constantine returned to Greece as king, but the military forced him to step down again in 1922. So it was that another son became King George II.

The Republic and the Dictatorship

In 1924, the military deposed King George II, and Greece declared itself a republic. The republic lasted until 1935, when George II was called back to power. However, the real power still rested with the military dictator General Joannes Metaxas. Greeks remember him for saying, *"Ochi!"* ("No!"). That was his answer on October 28, 1940, when Italian dictator Benito Mussolini demanded that Greece surrender to his invading forces. Greeks still celebrate October 28 as Ochi Day. That "no" dragged Greece into World War II (1939–1945) and led to Nazi Germany's occupation of the country from 1941 to 1944.

King George II went into exile during the war, but he returned in 1946, only to die a year later. Then his brother took the throne as King Paul I. After the devastation of the war years, Greece's economy picked up again. New

Development of Modern Greece, 1830–1947

■ Kingdom of Greece, 1830	■ Acquisitions, 1913
■ Acquisitions, 1863	■ Acquisitions, 1919
■ Acquisitions, 1881	■ Acquisitions after 1920

industries sprouted up, and farming expanded. When King Paul died in 1964, his son became King Constantine II.

Although Greek kings were political leaders, they did not have much governing power. The prime ministers actually ran the government. In the 1960s, prime minister George Papandreou charged that King Constantine was interfering in Greece's democratic government. This conflict soon led to political chaos.

Hoping to restore order, army officers seized the government in a military coup in 1967. King Constantine and the royal family fled the country and settled in England. Seven years of military dictatorship followed the coup, with General Georgios Papadopoulos in command. In 1973, Papadopoulos abolished the monarchy and declared Greece a republic.

General Georgios Papadopoulos, leader of the military dictatorship of Greece

Democracy Reborn

Democratic rule returned to Greece at last in 1974, with Konstantinos Karamanlis as prime minister and a new constitution as the law of the land. In the process, two new political parties emerged—the Panhellenic Socialist Movement (PASOK) and New Democracy parties.

Since then, leadership has passed between the two parties, with passionate issues on both sides. But one thing is certain—in the birthplace of democracy, democracy is here to stay.

Democracy at Work

GREEKS LIKE TO SAY THAT THEY INVENTED THE ART OF politics. They certainly invented democracy. Greece was the first nation in history to adopt democracy, or rule by the people, as its form of government.

Greece's official name is the Hellenic Republic. With the constitution of 1975, the nation declared itself a parliamentary democracy. Is Greece a democracy or a republic? Like many nations of the world, it is a democratic republic—a combination of both forms of government.

Opposite: **The changing of the guard outside the Parliament building in Athens**

City Hall, Corfu

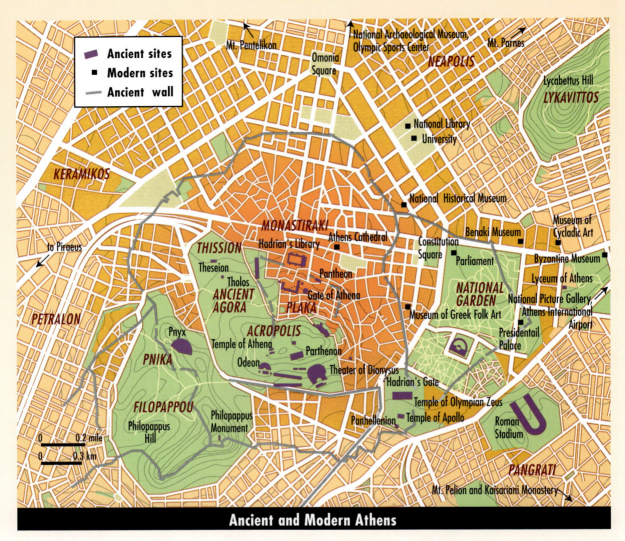

Ancient and Modern Athens

Legend:
- Ancient sites
- Modern sites
- Ancient wall

Map labels:
Mt. Pentelikon, National Archaeological Museum, Olympic Sports Center, Omonia Square, NEAPOLIS, Mt. Parnes, Lycabettus Hill, LYKAVITTOS, National Library, University, KERAMIKOS, National Historical Museum, Benaki Museum, Museum of Cycladic Art, MONASTIRAKI, THISSION, Hadrian's Library, Athens Cathedral, Constitution Square, Byzantine Museum, to Piraeus, Theseion, Pantheon, Parliament, Lyceum of Athens, Tholos, Gate of Athena, National Picture Gallery, ANCIENT AGORA, PLAKA, NATIONAL GARDEN, Athens International Airport, PETRALON, ACROPOLIS, Museum of Greek Folk Art, Pnyx, Temple of Athena, Parthenon, Presidentail Palace, PNIKA, Odeon, Theater of Dionysus, Hadrian's Gate, FILOPAPPOU, Temple of Olympian Zeus, Roman Stadium, Philopappus Hill, Philopappus Monument, Panhellenion, Temple of Apollo, PANGRATI, Mt. Pelion and Kaisariani Monastery

0   0.2 mile
0   0.3 km

Athens: The Capital City

Athens is the government, business, and cultural center of Greece. It's a modern metropolis, with steel-and-glass highrises and ferocious traffic. Yet reminders of Athens's past are everywhere. Around any corner might be an ancient monument or a Byzantine church.

About 770,000 people live in the city proper, and about 3.5 million people live in Athens's metropolitan area. Adding to the tight crunch of the resident population are more than 7 million tourists who visit every year.

At Athens's city center is Omonia Square. Just to the north is the National Archaeological Museum, housing countless archaeological treasures. Two broad avenues connect Omonia Square to Syntagma (Constitution) Square. Crowds gather there to watch the changing of

the guards at the Parliament building. Nearby is the National Garden, a cool, shady park.

High on a hill is the Acropolis, the most visited site in the country. On top of the Acropolis is Greece's most famous temple, the Parthenon (below). Across town

are Lycabettus Hill and Philopappus Hill, offering panoramic views of the city.

Clustered around the foot of the Acropolis are several unique districts. One is the Plaka, Athens's old town. Its cobblestone streets are lined with little shops and trendy cafés. Another is Monastiraki, a flea market jammed with clothing, jewelry, and knickknack stalls. Nearby is the ancient Agora. This was Athens's gathering place for merchants, philosophers, and politicians. Here, at their leisure, they hatched the ideas that would inspire democracies for ages to come.

Republics and Democracies

In a republic, power is in the hands of the people. It does not pass from parent to child—for instance, from a king to a prince. In calling itself the Hellenic Republic, Greece was taking a firm stand against monarchy.

The dream of democracy has led countless nations to throw off oppressive governments. Ancient Greece had a pure democracy. In a pure democracy, people elect leaders and make laws by direct votes. Many organizations today use this method to make decisions. New England's town hall meetings are one example. However, no national government today is a pure democracy.

If a nation has millions of voters, it's simply too difficult for everyone to vote on every single issue. That's why we have *representative* democracies. In this type of system, people elect representatives to speak for them. The business of government can move along much more smoothly that way.

The National Flag

In its upper left corner, the national flag of Greece features a white cross on a blue square. The cross is the traditional Greek Orthodox cross, with arms of equal length. Nine blue-and-white horizontal stripes cover the rest of the flag. The stripes stand for the nine syllables of the Greek patriots' motto, "*Eleutheria e Thanatos*," meaning "Freedom or Death." Blue and white are the national colors. Blue represents Greece's sea and sky, while white stands for the purity of the struggle for freedom. Greeks have used this flag since 1822.

In the United States, for example, voters from each state elect people to represent them in Congress. Likewise, voters in Greece elect representatives to their Parliament. That's why Greece is sometimes called a parliamentary democracy or a parliamentary republic.

The Legislature

The Vouli is Greece's Parliament. Its members make up the nation's legislative, or lawmaking, body. In many other countries, the legislature is bicameral, or composed of two houses—an upper house and a lower house. However, Greece's Parliament is unicameral; it has only one house.

Greece has 300 members of Parliament, and they are elected every four years. No one in Greece can choose not to vote. Voting is required by law for every citizen who is eighteen or older.

The Vouli meets at least once a year for a five-month session. When it passes a law, the president must either sign or veto that law. Parliament can override a veto with a vote of more than half its members.

Executive Powers

Greece's president is the head of state. The 1975 constitution also made the president the head of government. In 1986, new amendments to the constitution changed that role. Since then, the president's duties have been mostly symbolic and

National Anthem of Greece

Hymn to Freedom
Adopted in 1864
Words by Dionysos Solomós (1798–1857),
music by Nikolaos Mantzaros (1795–1873)

I shall always recognize you
By the dreadful sword you hold,
As the earth, with searching vision,
You survey, with spirit bold.
'Twas the Greeks of old whose dying
Brought to birth our spirit free.
Now, with ancient valor rising,
Let us hail you, oh Liberty!

ceremonial. Members of parliament elect the president to a five-year term. The president can be reelected only one time.

Greece's prime minister is the country's most powerful government leader, serving as the nation's chief executive and head of government. The president appoints the prime minister, but the choice is a clear one. The prime minister is usually the leader of the party that holds a majority of the seats in parliament at the time. With the prime minister's advice, the president also appoints a cabinet of about twenty ministers.

Judges and Courts

Greece's court system, like those of other European countries, arose out of ancient Roman law. The president appoints judges after consulting with a judicial council. All judges serve for life.

The Supreme Court and the Council of State are the two highest regular courts of law. The Supreme Court is the highest court for appeals in civil and criminal cases. The Council of State handles disputes over administration.

The Special Supreme Tribunal is in a class by itself. It decides whether a law or a court ruling is in line with the constitution. It also steps in to settle disputes over parliamentary elections.

Twelve Courts of Appeal rule on decisions appealed from lower civil and criminal courts. These cases would have started out in one of the fifty-nine Courts of First Instance. Other courts include juvenile courts and courts of the justice of the peace, as well as magistrates' courts, which are simple police courts.

Local Government

Greece is divided into thirteen traditional regions—nine on the mainland and four in the islands. For governing purposes, those regions are divided into fifty-one *nomoi*, or provinces. A fifty-second region, Mount Athos, is a self-governing district.

NATIONAL GOVERNMENT OF GREECE

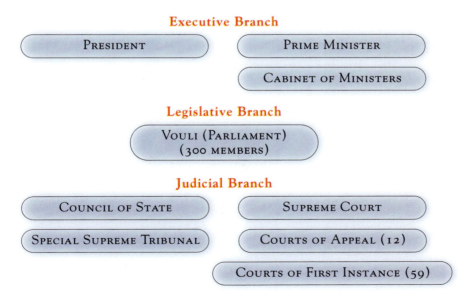

Executive Branch

PRESIDENT

PRIME MINISTER

CABINET OF MINISTERS

Legislative Branch

VOULI (PARLIAMENT)
(300 MEMBERS)

Judicial Branch

COUNCIL OF STATE

SUPREME COURT

SPECIAL SUPREME TRIBUNAL

COURTS OF APPEAL (12)

COURTS OF FIRST INSTANCE (59)

The national government appoints a *nomarch*, or governor, for each province. Nomarchs manage their provinces, keep order, and collect taxes. A special cabinet minister oversees the Greek provinces of Macedonia and Thrace.

Nomoi are divided into 147 smaller divisions called *eparchie*. They are like the counties in U.S. states. Cities, towns, and villages elect a mayor or president and a town council.

Political Parties

Greece has two major political parties: the Socialists and the Democrats. Their full names are the Panhellenic Socialist Movement (PASOK) and the New Democracy Party, respectively. Both were founded in 1974 after Greece's military dictatorship collapsed.

Socialists favor strong government controls on Greece's economy. They're concerned with social welfare and development, both for Greece and for its closest neighbors. Workers' rights and unemployment are often their major issues. Socialists are also wary of far-reaching international alliances.

Unlike Socialists, Democrats believe in a hands-off economic policy. They favor a free economy with few

Konstantinos Karamanlis

Konstantinos Karamanlis (1907–1998) was prime minister of Greece from 1955 to 1963 and from 1974 to 1980. He served as president from 1980 to 1985 and from 1990 to 1995.

Under Karamanlis, Greece enjoyed a quick economic recovery from World War II. In 1974, after the military dictatorship fell, Karamanlis restored a democratic government and founded the New Democracy Party. When his party lost its majority in 1980, Karamanlis moved from being prime minister to president. Thanks largely to his efforts, Greece joined the European Economic Union in 1981.

Andreas Papandreou

Andreas Papandreou (above left) (1919–1996) was prime minister of Greece from 1981 to 1989 and from 1993 to 1996. When the counry's military dictatorship collapsed in 1974, Papandreou returned to Greece and formed the Panhellenic Socialist Movement (PASOK). His popular party first gained a majority in parliament in 1981. Papandreou stepped down when PASOK lost its majority in 1989. However, he made a dramatic comeback in 1993 when he led his party to a land-slide victory.

government controls. They also focus on Greece's role among other Western nations. It was the Democrats of Greece who led the push for Greece's entry into the European Union.

Relations with Turkey

Greece has been at odds with its Turkish neighbors since the time of the Ottoman occupation. Relations between the two countries worsened in 1974. A dispute arose involving the island of Cyprus, a republic with centuries-long ties to Greece and whose population was 80 percent Greek. In 1974, Greek Cypriots overthrew their government, and Turkey invaded. Turks occupied about one-third of Cyprus and declared it the Turkish Republic of Northern Cyprus. As a result, as many as 200,000 Greek Cypriots became refugees. Greece still opposes a divided Cyprus. However, the two countries have begun peaceful talks on the issue.

Another ongoing dispute has to do with territorial waters. Turkey claims more rights in the Aegean Sea than Greece wishes to accept. This includes shipping space and offshore oil-drilling rights. Tensions increased in 1996 when Turkey

Turkish soldiers after the invasion of Cyprus

laid claim to the Imia island group in the Aegean Sea. These islands are believed to contain petroleum deposits.

Relations with Macedonia

The name "Macedonia" refers to many things. It's a geographic region, an ancient kingdom, and two political regions—all with different boundaries. If it had not been the birthplace of Alexander the Great, Macedonia might not be as well-known as it is today. After the Balkan Wars of 1912–1913, Macedonia was divided between Greece and Yugoslavia.

When Yugoslavia broke apart in 1991, its republics became separate, independent nations. One of them was Yugoslavia's portion of the divided Macedonia. As an independent republic, it called itself the Federal Socialist Republic of Macedonia. For its national flag, it adopted the 16-pointed Star of Vergina, which Alexander the Great had used.

Greece immediately objected to both the name and the flag. Macedonia is a Greek name, Greece insisted, and Alexander the Great is a Greek national hero. The Greeks also distrusted the new republic's constitution. They believed it suggested that the Greek province of Macedonia belonged to the present-day republic of Macedonia. In Greece's view, this might indicate an intention to make claims on Greece's national territory.

In 1993, the United Nations suggested the temporary title of Former Yugoslav Republic of Macedonia, or FYROM. Greece grudgingly agreed. In 1995, FYROM removed the Vergina symbol from its flag. The two countries are slowly improving their relations.

Making a Living

GREECE'S ECONOMY WAS IN SHAMBLES AT THE END OF World War II. Since then, it has made an amazing comeback. Government programs had a lot to do with this recovery.

Today, about 20 percent of the workers in Greece hold government jobs. They include teachers, medical workers, tour guides, and many other professionals. The government still controls many of Greece's industries, but it is gradually turning them over to private owners.

Opposite: **A police officer at work**

Greece's medical workers are employed by the government.

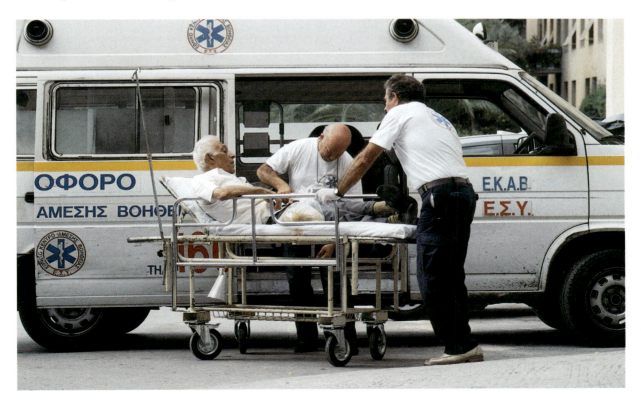

Weights and Measures

Greece, like most European countries, uses the metric system for weights and measures.

Joining the EU in 1981 also boosted Greece's economy. The EU opened up more opportunities for trade with other European countries. As a member of the EU, Greece also receives aid for agriculture, road building, and many other projects.

Still, Greece's economy lags behind that of other EU countries. For example, salaries in Greece are much lower than those in the rest of Europe. The minimum wage for Greek workers is equal to about U.S.$390 a month. In contrast, France's minimum wage is the equivalent of about U.S.$850 a month, and the United Kingdom's is the equivalent of about U.S.$875. About 10 percent of a Greek worker's pay is taken for taxes and another 10 percent for national health care. The government provides free hospitals and other medical services. Greek workers also get at least one month of paid vacation every year.

About 10 percent of Greek adults are unemployed. Many of them are university graduates. Even with a college education,

What Does It Cost?

Here are several common food products and their prices:

Product	Price (in Greek Drachmas)	Price (in Euros)	Equivalent (in U.S.$)*
Potato chips, medium bag	220	.65	.56
Milk, liter	172	.50	.44
Bread, loaf	155	.45	.40
Soft drink, can	350	1.03	.89
Milk shake, large	450	1.32	1.15
Gum, pack	170	.50	.43

*Equivalents based on 391 drachmas/1.15 Euros to $1.00 U.S. (February 2002)

Good-Bye to the Drachma

The drachma—2,650 years old—was Europe's oldest currency. The Athenian drachma of the sixth century B.C. was a silver coin that became standard currency throughout much of Europe and Asia. However, Greece, like most of Europe, has adopted the Euro as its national currency. As of 2002, the drachma was officially out of use. For old times' sake, here is information on the drachma.

One drachma was made up of 100 lepta. The value of the lepta was so small that it was rarely used. Bank notes came in denominations of 10,000, 5,000, 1,000, 500, 200, 100, and 50 drachmas. Coins came in values of 100, 50, 20, 10, and (very rarely) 5 drachmas.

One hundred drachmas equaled about 26 U.S. cents in February 2002. In the same time period, one Euro was equal to about 341 drachmas or about 87 U.S. cents.

it's hard to find a job. Graduates often find themselves working in service jobs until they can land a job in their field.

Children often add to the family income, too. By law, they can work beginning at age fifteen. Twelve-year-olds can work in a family business, and many younger children work for family farms and restaurants. "Street kids" sell flowers, packets of tissues, and other items. Many of these children are Albanian immigrants. Others are Gypsies, a migratory people who tend to live on the fringes of settled society.

Olive harvesting techniques have stayed the same for generations.

Working the Land

Dry, rocky land makes raising crops difficult in Greece. However, olive trees thrive there. Their long roots reach deep into the soil, where underground water is trapped.

Ancient Greek paintings show fascinating scenes of olive harvests. Greeks today harvest olives the same way their ancestors did. They lay nets or tarpaulins on the ground under the trees. Then they beat the branches with long sticks, and the olives fall down into the nets.

Greece is one of the world's largest producers of olives and olive oil. Harvesting begins in the fall and takes place in "shifts." Green olives for the table are harvested in September and October, whereas black olives are gathered from November through January. The last to go are the olives to be pressed for olive oil. It takes four to five liters of olives to make one liter of olive oil.

In Greek mythology, the goddess Demeter taught the world how to cultivate grain. Her Roman name, Ceres, gave us the word "cereal." Demeter would be pleased to know that wheat is now Greece's major crop. Although Greece's soil is generally poor, wheat and other field crops thrive on the rich plains of Thessaly, Macedonia, and Thrace.

Harvesting tobacco leaves

Greeks enjoy plenty of fresh, locally grown fruits and vegetables. They raise grapes, melons, peaches, corn, tomatoes, lemons, and oranges. The grapes are made into wine or sold as raisins. Greece is also a major producer of cotton and tobacco for the EU countries.

What Greece Grows, Makes, and Mines

Agriculture (1998)

Tomatoes	2,085,000 metric tons
Olives	2,068,000 metric tons
Wheat	2,058,000 metric tons
Sugar beets	1,996,000 metric tons

Manufacturing *(exports by $millions U.S.)*

Manufactured goods (total)	$7,923
Food products	$1,219
Petroleum products	$619

Mining

Bauxite	2,168,000 metric tons
Iron ore	810,000 metric tons
Gypsum	795,000 metric tons

Orange and lemon trees add a bright touch to parks, city avenues, country roadsides, and private yards. More than just a food source, they're prized as decorative trees. The oranges are bitter oranges, not the sweet variety. They're good mainly for making marmalade.

Orange trees grow along roadsides, in private yards, and in busy cities.

A shepherd watches over his herd as it grazes.

Shepherds with their goats or sheep are a familiar sight around the hilly countryside. Chickens and guinea fowl are the most common farm animals. They and their eggs end up in the markets and on family dinner tables.

Manufacturing

Food and food products are Greece's leading manufactured goods. Bread, dried fruits, canned nuts, packaged meat, dairy products, and wine are some of the country's processed foods. Next in importance are metal products, textiles, clothing, and petroleum products.

Handcrafted traditional textiles at an open-air market

This woman paints a traditional design on a pot in a workshop in Rhodes. She will add the colors at a later stage.

About 15 percent of the Greek labor force work in manufacturing, but that figure represents only factory workers. Many people produce handmade items in their homes. They make cotton and wool textiles, yarn, clothes, leather goods, jewelry, ceramics, and other products they can sell in the markets.

Pottery was a fine art in ancient Greece. Today, ceramics is a growing industry. Skilled craft workers spin their creations on pottery wheels and decorate them with delicate, colorful traditional patterns. Many islands and regions have their own distinctive pottery styles, and some cities have huge ceramics workshops.

Mining

Mining is a small but important industry in Greece. Bauxite is the most valuable metal. Greek refineries use it to make aluminum. Lignite, a type of coal, is another major mining product. Most of it is burned in power plants to generate electricity. Chromite is another important mineral, used in making stainless steel.

Greece has small deposits of uranium, natural gas, and petroleum. The petroleum is in the undersea Prinos field, near the Aegean island of Thanos. This petroleum bed—and the possibility of others—is one of the reasons that Greece and Turkey argue so heatedly over territorial rights in the Aegean.

Ancient Greeks used marble to build statues and temples. Marble for the Parthenon came from quarries on

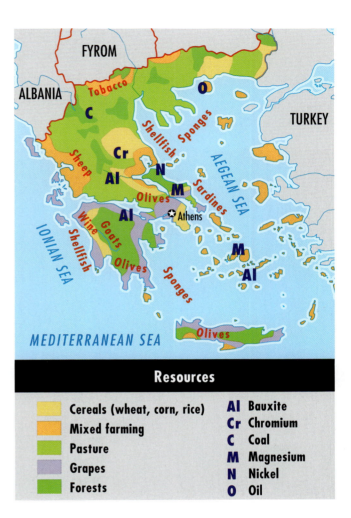

Resources

Cereals (wheat, corn, rice)	**Al** Bauxite
Mixed farming	**Cr** Chromium
Pasture	**C** Coal
Grapes	**M** Magnesium
Forests	**N** Nickel
	O Oil

Marble

Marble begins as limestone. Under pressure and heat, the limestone molecules are recrystallized, or reshaped, into marble. Fine-grained marble is preferred for sculptures, while coarse-grained marble is better for less delicate uses. When various minerals are present in the marble, they produce different colors. Marble might be white, red, yellow, brown, grey, pink, green, black, or a swirly mixture of colors.

Mount Pentelikon. Mule teams hauled the 12-ton marble blocks down one mountain and up the other. Today, any public or private building in Greece might have marble floors, stair steps, columns, or walls. About 7 percent of all the marble produced in the world comes from Greece.

Blocks of marble being quarried in the Cyclades

Fishing

Fresh *kalamári*, or squid, comes right from the Aegean Sea to the table. Greek fishermen catch lobster, shrimp, and a variety of fishes, too. Fishing has always been important to Greece's economy. Any stretch of coastline is likely to be bristling with fishing boats—from big commercial trawlers to small, wooden rowboats.

More than half of all the sea bass and sea bream caught in the European Union come from Greece. Fishermen also haul in hefty loads of sardines, mackerel, and anchovies. Most commercial fishing takes place in the coastal waters of the Aegean Sea. With the help of the EU, Greece is also building inland lagoons for "farm-raised" fish. The lagoons hold trout, sturgeon, carp, and eels, as well as sea bream and sea bass.

Masters of the Sea

Throughout their history, Greeks have loved the sea—both for its beauty and for the freedom it offers them. Hercules, Jason, and other mythological seafarers live on in Greece as inspiring heroes.

Greeks mastered the seas thousands of years ago. King Minos of Crete built a navy that ruled the Mediterranean. Cretan seamen were bold pirates, too. Piracy was considered an honorable profession then. A pirate had to have the same qualities as a good soldier. He was bold, fearless, and faithful, and was an expert seaman.

Themistocles set up Athens's harbor of Piraeus in the fifth century B.C. Athens soon became a powerful center both for

A view of the harbor in Piraeus filled with merchant ships

Cars board ferries on a daily basis in Greece.

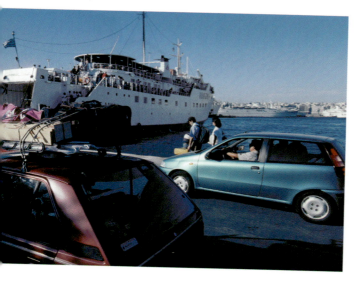

warships and trading vessels. The city-state collected taxes from all incoming vessels. Merchants and shipowners of Athens became wealthy from their trading ventures to Italy, Africa, and Russia. Today, Piraeus is still Greece's major port.

With more than 1,800 merchant ships in service, Greece has one of the largest fleets in the world. Some of the world's wealthiest people belong to Greek families who made their fortunes in shipping. Aristotle Onassis and Stavros Niarchos are some of the better-known shipping businessmen, but there are hundreds of others.

Smaller vessels are part of Greece's everyday transportation system. Ferries carry people, cars, and trucks between Greece and Italy. Ferries also run between the mainland and the major islands of Greece. For some people, the ferry is their means of commuting to work.

The Corinth Canal

The people of ancient Corinth had a great idea. Ships had to sail all the way around the Peloponnese Peninsula to get from the Ionian Sea to the Aegean Sea. So the Corinthians offered a service that was too good to turn down. They laid a "road" of logs across the isthmus of Corinth—the narrow strip of land connecting the peninsula to the mainland. For a fee, they would haul ships from one side to the other. The ships rolled along on the logs as men trudged ahead pulling ropes tied to the ships.

Later, the Roman emperor Nero hatched the idea of cutting through the isthmus to make a canal. However, he ran into a religious problem. The sea level of the Ionian Sea was higher than the Aegean. Nero was afraid that connecting the two would upset the balance of nature and thus anger the gods.

Modern shipping needs won out in the end. French, German, and Greek teams built the Corinth Canal between 1882 and 1893. Then ships could take the canal and cut right through the heart of Greece.

The Corinth Canal is 4 miles (6.4 km) long and 80 feet (24 m) wide. Its walls are 240 feet (73 m) high.

Large commercial ships no longer use the canal, though, because it's too shallow and narrow. Only cruise ships and smaller vessels do.

Getting Around

Drive along any highway or country road in Greece and you will see roadside shrines. They look like little churches with crosses on top. Each one marks the spot of a car accident. Relatives of the accident victims erect the shrines to commemorate their loved ones and gain blessings for them. Inside each tiny shrine is either a picture of the victim or an image of a saint. Greece has the highest rate of deadly highway accidents in Europe. This is in part because many people don't buckle their seat belts.

Roads in Greece wind around mountains, cut through valleys, and line the coasts. Steep, rocky hillsides and cliffs often loom along the roadsides. Railroads, too, must snake around the mountainous terrain.

Athens's new subway train, the Athens Metro, is fast and low-priced. Some people say it's one of the best museums in Athens. Each Metro station has interesting history, archaeology, or art exhibits. The station at Syntagma Square, for example, features a cutaway view of an excavation showing the periods of Greek history.

It wasn't easy to build Athens's new airport. Engineers had to flatten a hill and relocate a fifteenth-century Greek Orthodox church. Finally, the Athens International Airport opened in spring 2001—just in time for the tourist season. The airport's official name is Eleftherios Venizelos, named for the Cretan statesman.

Greece has more international airports than most countries. That's because so many foreign tourists want to visit. The islands of Crete, Corfu, Rhodes, Cos, and Lesbos, and the mainland cities of Alexandroupolis and Andravida all

A tourist views an archaeological excavation in the Metro station at Syntagma Square.

have international airports. Olympic Airways is the national airline of Greece.

Keeping in Touch

It's easy to use the Internet in Greece. Just stop into an Internet café, pay a small per-minute fee, and log on. For people who can't afford a computer, it's a great way to send and receive messages and cruise the Web. Although some Internet cafés just provide Internet services, others are also real cafés with snacks and drinks.

Until the 1980s, the government owned Greece's radio and television networks. Naturally, they reported the news with a pro-government view. Now all opinions are freely aired on Greece's many privately owned stations.

Newspapers, too, opened up in the 1980s. Today they brandish their political opinions freely. More than 100 daily and weekly news-papers keep Greeks up to date on the news. *Eleftheros Typos (Free Press)* is the largest daily newspaper, followed by *Ta Nea (News)* and *Eleftherotypia (Press Freedom)*. *Athens News* is the country's leading English-language newspaper.

A newspaper stand displays the day's headlines.

People, Language, and Learning

While most Greeks prefer urban living, this woman dwells in the country.

Opposite: **Zappeion Park in Athens**

ALTHOUGH GREECE IS A SMALL COUNTRY, it has plenty of room for everyone. On average, there are about 206 people per square mile (80 per sq km). If Greeks were spread out evenly across the country, every man, woman, and child would have almost three football fields for a living space! This is far from the reality, however.

Almost two-thirds of the people live in cities and towns, while the rest live in the countryside. Settlement is sparse in the high mountains. Only scattered villages lie in the mountainous center of the mainland and the highlands of the Peloponnese. As in ancient times, people tend to cluster along the seacoasts.

About 10.9 million people live in Greece, according to the 2001 census. Athens, the capital, is the largest city. With its

A bustling street in Athens

Ethnic Mix	
Greek	98%
Other	2%

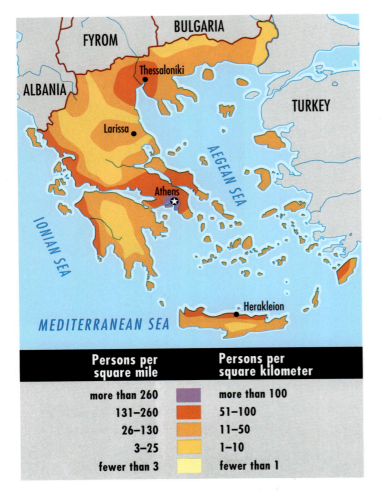

Persons per square mile		Persons per square kilometer
more than 260		more than 100
131–260		51–100
26–130		11–50
3–25		1–10
fewer than 3		fewer than 1

Where People Live

Athens (city only)	772,072
Thessaloniki (city only)	383,967
Piraeus	182,671
Patras	153,344
Herakleion	116,178

(1991 census figures)

congested traffic and tight living spaces, it seems to be bursting at the seams. Athens's metropolitan area is home to more than 3 million people. That's nearly one-third of the country's entire population!

Thessaloniki is the second-largest city, with a metropolitan population of about 740,000 people. It's the capital of Greece's Macedonia region, as well as an industrial center and an important Aegean port city. Piraeus, Athens's port city, is the third-largest city, and Patras, on the north coast of the Peloponnese, is the fourth-largest.

About 98 percent of the people in Greece are ethnic Greeks. They consider their ancestors prehistoric settlers of the second millennium B.C. Turks form the largest minority group. Other minorities are Albanians, Macedonians, Bulgarians, Armenians, and Gypsies.

The Language: A Battleground

In ancient times, Greeks in different regions spoke different dialects. For example, they spoke Attic in Athens, Doric in parts of the Peloponnese, and Ionic in many of the islands.

Attic, or Hellenistic Greek, became the major language of the Golden Age.

After the conquests of Alexander the Great, Hellenistic Greek spread throughout the Middle East. It became the common language for business and learning. Along the way, foreign words were mixed in. This mixed version of Greek was called *Koine*. Under the Byzantine Empire, Koine became the official language of the government and the Orthodox Church.

During the independence movement, some Greek scholars set out to "purify" the language. They removed all foreign words to create a form of Greek called *katharevusa*. It became the official language of the new nation. Meanwhile,

Two men pause for a chat.

Common Greek Phrases

Greek	Pronunciation	English
kaliméra	kah-lee-MEH-rah	good day
kalispéra	kah-lee-SPEH-rah	good evening
kaliníkhta	kah-lee-NEEK-tah	good night
ne	neh (turn head to side)	yes
ochi	OH-shee (jerk head upward)	no
parakaló	pah-rah-kah-LOH	please
efkharistó	ef-kah-rees-TOH	thank you
ti kanis?	tee KAH-nees	how are you?

The Greek Alphabet

Cap.	Small	Name	English Equivalent
Α	α	alpha	a as in "father"
Β	β	beta	b
Γ	γ	gamma	g as in "get"
Δ	∂	delta	d
Ε	ε	epsilon	e as in "egg"
Ζ	ζ	zeta	z—say like ds as in "toads"
Η	η	eta	e—say like ey as in "hey"
Θ	θ	theta	th as in "thin"
Ι	ι	iota	i—say like ee as in "meet"
Κ	κ	kappa	k
Λ	λ	lambda	l
Μ	μ	mu	m
Ν	ν	nu	n
Ξ	ξ	xi	x as in "box"
Ο	ο	omicron	o as in "top"
Π	π	pi	p
Ρ	ρ	rho	r
Σ	σ	sigma	s
Τ	τ	tau	t
Υ	υ	upsilon	u as in "put"
Φ	φ	phi	f
Χ	χ	chi	ch as in "Loch Ness"
Ψ	ψ	psi	ps as in "lapse"
Ω	ω	omega	o as in "toe"

ordinary people still spoke the common language, called demotic (*dhimotiki*). By the 1970s, katharevusa had lost its appeal and demotic Greek became Greece's official language.

Greek Is Everywhere!

Today, about 12 million people around the world speak Greek. They live in Greece and Cyprus, Italy, Albania, Turkey, the United States, and many other countries. People in some regions of Greece still speak traditional dialects, though.

Written Greek had a smoother history than the spoken language did. Mycenaeans used a written language as early as the thirteenth century B.C. They wrote in a script called Linear B. In the eighth century B.C., Greeks began using a script based on the Phoenician alphabet. This script is the ancestor of the modern Greek alphabet, which has twenty-four letters.

Thousands of English words came from the Greek language. In some cases, the Romans adopted a Greek word into Latin before it made its way into English. We've adopted certain letters of the Greek alphabet, too. "Alphabet" itself comes from *alpha* and *beta*, the Greek alphabet's

first two letters. The letter *delta* (*d*) is shaped like a triangle, and we use the word "delta" for the triangular pattern of streams at a river's mouth. *Gamma, pi,* and other Greek letters are universal mathematical symbols.

Some Greek letters are similar to those in the Latin alphabet, although they may represent different sounds.

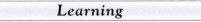

Learning

As farmers labor in their fields, many of them dream of their child becoming a doctor or a lawyer someday. A good education is prized in Greece. It's not only honorable, but it also helps a person to move up in society. Wealthy Greeks donate generously to schools and universities. In the 1950s, only about 30 percent of Greek adults could read and write. Now, thanks to aggressive education programs, the literacy rate is more than 95 percent.

Some English Words That Came from Greek

English	Greek Originial
academy	*Akademeia* (the school where Plato taught)
acoustics	*akoustikos* (having to do with hearing)
acrobat	*akrobatos* (walking up high)
chronological	*chronikos* (having to do with time) + *logos* (reason)
church	*kyrios* (lord, master)
cosmetics	*kosmetikos* (skilled in adornment)
dialogue	*dialegesthai* (to converse)
dynamic	*dynamikos* (powerful)
echo	*eche* (sound)
electronic	*elektron*, from *elektor* (beaming sun)
epistle	*epistole* (message, letter)
ethnic	*ethnos* (a nation or people)
fantastic	*phantastikos* (producing mental images)
hypnosis	*hypnos* (sleep)
idea	*eidenai* (to know), *idein* (to see)
logical	*logos* (reason)
melody	*meloidia* (chanting, music)
metropolis	*metropolis*, from *meter* (mother) + *polis* (city)
mystery	*mysterion*, from *mystos* (keeping silence)
myth	*mythos* (myth)
pathetic	*pathetikos* (capable of feeling emotion)
patriot	*patrios* (having to do with one's father)
philosophy	*philos* (beloved) + *sophia* (wisdom)
politics	*politikos* (political), *polites* (citizen)
zoo	*zoe* (life)

Greece offers free public education at all levels. Children are required to attend school from age six through age fifteen. They spend six years in primary school (*dimotiko skholeio*) and another six years in secondary school (*gymnasio*). The school year is divided into three equal cycles. Many public school students also attend private schools called *frontistiria* in the evenings. There they get extra coaching for their college entrance exams.

Students face stiff competition when they try to get into universities. Many students study outside the country because Greece has only sixteen colleges and universities. The University of Athens and the Aristotelian University in Thessaloniki are the largest. There are also schools of archaeology and universities of political science, economics, agriculture, art, and industrial research.

Greek students learning jewelry design

Spiritual Lives

Church overlooking the sea in the Peloponnese

Greece, like all free societies, grants freedom of worship to all of its people. Most Greeks, however, are members of the Greek Orthodox Church, the nation's official religion. In fact, about 98 percent of Greeks belong to the Greek Orthodox faith.

Greek Orthodoxy reinforces Greeks' sense of national identity and solidarity. Religious festivals are a deep-seated part of Greek culture, and the church touches many areas of public and private life. The church's effort to stay relevant in modern times has also helped keep it popular.

Opposite: **Fresco of the Virgin Mary with the Christ child in the Agios Demetrios Cathedral**

Religions in Greece	
Greek Orthodox	98%
Muslim	1.3%
All Others	0.7%

Muslims are the largest religious minority. They make up a little more than 1 percent of the population. Most are ethnic Turks who live in western Thrace and the Dodecanese Islands. Small communities of Roman Catholics, Protestants, and Jews also live in Greece.

The Greek Orthodox Church—also called the Church of Greece—is one of several Eastern Orthodox churches. They all share the same basic beliefs and many similar traditions. Greek Orthodoxy is self-governing; that is, it is not subject to a higher authority. Its head, called the primate of Greece, is the archbishop of Athens.

The people of Crete belong to their own branch of Greek Orthodoxy. Their religious leader is the archbishop of Crete. Mount Athos and the Dodecanese Islands are separate, too. They are subject to the patriarch of Constantinople and not to the archbishop of Athens.

The First European Christians

Greece was the center of many exciting events in the early years of Christianity. St. Paul lived and preached in Greece for many years. In fact, Philippi was the first site in Europe where he preached and set up a Christian community. From Philippi, he moved on to Thessaloniki.

In Athens, Paul preached from atop the Areopagus—the massive stone at the base of the Acropolis. Then he made Corinth his headquarters for a year and a half. Other trips took him to the Aegean Islands, as well as Ephesus, the Greek city on the Turkish coast. After he left Greece, he wrote epistles, or letters of instruction and encouragement, to Christian communities in Greece. Anyone familiar with the Christian Bible has read Paul's letters to the Philippians, Thessalonians, Corinthians, and Ephesians.

Patriarchs, Metropolitans, and Priests

During the Byzantine and Ottoman eras, the Greek Orthodox Church was under the rule of the patriarch of Constantinople. After independence, however, Greece's new government was afraid that Turkey might still try to control Greece through the patriarch. The Greek Church therefore declared itself independent in 1833. Constantinople finally agreed to independence in 1850. Since then, the Greek Orthodox Church has governed itself and appointed its own bishops.

The archbishop of Athens presides over a synod, or council, of twelve metropolitans (bishops of major cities). They help run the day-to-day affairs of the church. The archdiocese is divided into seventy-eight dioceses, with a bishop overseeing each one.

Archbishop Christodoulos

The official title of Christodoulos Paraskevaides is His Beatitude Christodoulos, Archbishop of Athens and All of Greece. He was born in 1939 at Xanthi in Thrace and earned degrees in law, French, and English, as well as a doctorate in theology. Christodoulos was elected Metropolitan of Demetrias in 1974 and Archbishop of Athens and All of Greece in 1998. He has met with religious and political leaders all over the world and has spoken out against racism, terrorism, and military aggression.

Priests wear a long, black robe (*soutane*), a round, high hat (*skoufia*), long hair, and a beard. To become a priest, a young man studies theology for at least two years. Those who hope to be a bishop one day also take further studies at the universities of Athens or Thessaloniki.

Greek Orthodox priests may marry, but only before they have taken their final vows. However, only unmarried priests can rise up into the higher ranks of the Church. Since Greek Orthodoxy is the state religion, the Greek government pays priests' salaries. The pay is rather low, so many priests have to take second jobs.

Beliefs and Practices

Like all Eastern Orthodox faiths, Greek Orthodoxy claims apostolic succession. This means that the authority of its patriarchs follows in an unbroken chain from the time of the apostles until today. Greek Orthodox services use the Greek Koine language of the Byzantine Era. They follow the Byzantine rite, an ancient set of ceremonies rich with symbolism. Services include incense burning and magnificent chanting.

The congregation stands during the church service, with women on the left and

Selected Religious Holidays

St. Basil's Day	January 1
Epiphany	January 6
Apokries (Carnival Sunday)	Sunday before Lent begins
Easter Week	date varies
St. George's Day	April 23
Analipsi (Ascension)	40 days after Easter
Pentikosti (Pentecost)	50 days after Easter
Metamorfosi (Transfiguration)	August 6
Dormition (Assumption) of the Virgin Mary	August 15
St. Demetrios's Day	October 26
St. Nicholas's Day	December 6
Christmas	December 25 and 26

men on the right. In making the sign of the cross, they touch the forehead, the chest, and the right shoulder before the left. The first three fingers are held together, symbolizing the Trinity—God the Father, Son, and Holy Spirit.

The worship service begins with the priest entering the church in procession. Next comes a series of scripture readings. Another procession leads to a reading of the Creed, or profession of beliefs, the consecration of bread and wine, and Communion, one of the seven sacraments. The faithful receive Communion in the forms of bread and wine.

When infants are baptized, they are dipped in water three times. After baptism, a baby also receives the sacraments of Chrismation (Confirmation, or anointing with oil) and Communion. In weddings, the bride and groom are crowned with white wreaths joined by a ribbon. This signifies that they are joined as a new family in the sight of God. Then they drink from a common cup, showing they share the burdens and joys of their new life together.

A Greek wedding ceremony is rich with symbolism.

Religious festivals are an important part of Greek culture. Most Greeks attend church services on Easter—the most important feast of the year—and Christmas. Other church-going occasions are the feasts of village patron saints and of saints who are beloved nationwide. Church services are followed by eating, drinking, singing, and dancing.

Icons and Church Designs

Greek Orthodox churches are richly adorned with icons—gold-highlighted paintings of Christ, the Virgin Mary, and the saints. Icons are also used in homes and shrines. In a church, icons hang on the iconostasis. This is a screen that separates the congregation from the sanctuary, where the priest presides.

Traditional icon subjects are the Preparation—an empty throne awaiting Christ's return—and the Dormition—the Virgin's ascent into heaven. Favorite saints include St. George, St. Andrew of Patras, St. Demetrios of Thessaloniki, St. Michael, St. Nicholas, St. John the Baptist, and the Three Hierarchs—Saints John Chrysostom, Basil, and Gregory.

The typical Greek Orthodox church is built in the Byzantine style. It's designed in the shape of a Greek cross, with four equal-sized arms. Over the center rises a massive dome, symbolizing the vault of heaven, with a cross on top.

A shrine with an icon of the Virgin Mary

Monks and Monasteries

Monks are men who belong to a monastery, or spiritual community. They take vows of poverty, chastity, and obedience. Greece has more than 200 monasteries, many of which are more than one thousand years old. In the more conservative monasteries, daily life is a combination of prayer, fasting, and rigorous discipline. Because monks don't marry, most of the church's metropolitans are monks.

Some monasteries house communities of nuns—women dedicated to a spiritual life. These communities are called convents in some other countries, but they're known as monasteries in Greece. Many of them operate schools, orphanages, and medical centers.

Countless monasteries were founded during the Byzantine period. Each one featured several buildings, often including a fine library, a bakery, and an oil press. Many monks were scholars who translated ancient Greek works into the Byzantine dialect.

Mount Athos and Meteora are Greece's most famous monasteries. Mount Athos is a community of twenty monasteries situated on a mountaintop on Macedonia's Chalcidice Peninsula. Monks first settled there in the ninth century A.D., and more than one thousand live there today. Now it houses beautiful paintings, icons, and manuscripts. Only men can visit Mount Athos, and only with special permission.

Meteora, a group of monasteries in western Thessaly, is an awesome sight. Twenty-four towering pillars of rock rise straight up above the plains, and perched high on their craggy summits are monasteries. Monks built them in the 1300s

Iconoclasm

In 726, Emperor Leo III introduced a policy of iconoclasm ("the breaking of icons"). He ordered all icons destroyed, charging that using icons was idolatry, or worshiping an object as a god. This policy lasted until 843, when Empress Theodora restored icons. Today the word "iconoclast" means someone who attacks established beliefs or institutions.

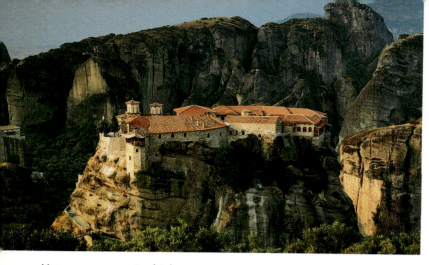

Meteora monasteries high on pillars of rock in Thessaly

and named their community Meteora, meaning "hanging in the air."

East Versus West

Today's Greek Orthodox Church has had a long and stormy history. In the fourth century A.D., Christianity had five major centers, each headed by a patriarch. The patriarchs of Rome and Constantinople had an uneasy relationship, for each one felt he was Christianity's principal leader. Nevertheless, they agreed on basic beliefs. Church councils in Nicaea (325 A.D.) and Constantinople (381 A.D.) drew up a creed—a statement of Christian beliefs—that all the patriarchs accepted.

During the following century, the Western Roman Empire collapsed. In the 800s, the Holy Roman Empire was established, with Rome as its capital. Politics and religion were closely intertwined, and religious leaders in Rome and Constantinople began to lock horns in earnest. Eastern and Western Christianity finally split in 1054. It happened over one Latin word—*filioque*, meaning "and the Son."

The Filioque Issue

The filioque issue was about the place of the Holy Spirit within the Holy Trinity. Church leaders had agreed on a creed in the 300s. It stated that both the Son and the Holy Spirit "proceed" from the Father. This means that the Father is the source of the other two—the one who gives them their meaning. In 431, the church council of Ephesus declared that the creed could not be changed.

In the 800s, however, the church in Rome added the word "filioque" to the creed. The change in wording changed its meaning. This new version meant that the Holy Spirit proceeds not just "from the Father" but "from the Father and the Son." It therefore changed the way of looking at the relationship among the three. To the Eastern Church, this change produced two wrongs: (1) it went against the Council of Ephesus; and (2) it changed the proper understanding of the Trinity.

Archbishop Christodoulos meets with Pope John Paul II.

The filioque debate went on for another 200 years. In 1054, the pope—head of the Roman Church—sent a delegate to the patriarch of Constantinople, but the patriarch refused to see him. As a result, the Roman delegate excommunicated the patriarch—that is, he declared him no longer a member of the Church. The patriarch, in turn, condemned the delegate. This was the final split.

In 1965, more than 900 years later, Patriarch Athenagoras and Pope Paul VI mutually canceled the condemnations. In 2001, Pope John Paul II addressed Greek Archbishop Christodoulos and expressed regret for Catholics' past sins against Orthodox Christians. This was partly a reference to the shameful Fourth Crusade. The faithful on both sides, however, doubt that the two churches will ever reunite.

Traditions That Never Die

GREEK ARTS, CULTURE, AND SPORTS HAVE THEIR ROOTS in the past. They may recall time-honored folk customs, the struggle for independence, or the glories of the ancient world.

Folk music and traditional dances are part of every festive occasion in Greece, from religious feasts to family gatherings and weddings. Each region has its own characteristic style.

Greeks all over the world dance the *kalamatianos*. It originated in the olive-growing Kalamata province. To celebrate a rich harvest, the women used to take off their scarves and wave them as they whirled around in a circle. This dance also recalls the brave Souliot women. Fleeing the Turk Ali Pasha in 1803, they danced the kalamatianos upon a cliff. Then they flung themselves and their children over the edge rather than be captured.

Two other popular dances, the *zembetiko* and *hassapiko*, are of Middle Eastern origin. They're performed by men in wide-sleeved white shirts. Out of the hassapiko grew the popular *syrtaki* dances. Here, the leader dances ever more challenging variations and the next man must duplicate them. The *pentozali*, from Crete, imitates actions of men in battle. The dancers wear knee boots, black pants, and headscarves.

Opposite: **Traditional Greek women's folk dance**

A men's traditional folk dance

The Greek *rebetikos* are much like the blues in the United States. They're songs of the urban poor. Other folk songs descended from medieval Byzantine music and so have a Middle Eastern flavor. *Kleftikos* are typical songs in this style. They're plaintive songs of the Klephts—heroic peasant bandits who fought the Ottomans in the struggle for independence.

The *bouzouki* is the main instrument for folk music. It's a sort of fat-bodied guitar. Another folk instrument is a three-stringed lyre played with a bow. The *zournas*, a type of oboe, used to give folk music its sharp, piercing melody lines. Now most folk bands use a clarinet instead. The *sandouri* is a rectangular instrument that lays flat as the player strikes its strings with sticks. It's a descendant of the psaltery, an ancient musical instrument mentioned in the Bible.

This man plays the guitar-like bouzouki.

Some early Greek folk instruments were shepherds' flutes made from reeds, wood, or animal bones. Goat herders would join in, playing harmony with bells from their goats' necks. This gentle image is a far cry from today's popular Greek music. Now even the traditional instruments are electrified and amplified.

Many modern Greek composers are known worldwide. Mikis Theodorakis used the melodies and rhythms of rebetika

Maria Callas

Greece's favorite opera star was the prima donna Maria Callas (1923–1977). Originally named Maria Kalogeropoulos, she was born in New York City to Greek emigrants. At thirteen, she moved to Athens with her mother and studied singing. She made her first professional appearance at age fifteen and became an international sensation at age twenty-four. The public loved Callas, and the popular press kept track of her flamboyant temper and her romantic adventures.

songs in his compositions. He wrote the film score for *Zorba the Greek*. Dimitris Metropoulos was both a composer and the director of the Athens Symphony Orchestra. Famous for his memory, Metropoulos conducted without a musical score.

Goat-Songs and Revels

The first tragedies honored Dionysus, the god of wine, and the players wore goatskins. That's why the word tragedy means "goat-song." Greek tragedies were noble stories of gods, kings, and heroes. In contrast, comedies were about lower-class characters and their antics. Thus, "comedy" comes from the word meaning "revel." Those meanings have changed, however. Today, a comedy is a play with a happy ending, and a tragedy is one that ends sadly.

The ancient theater at Epidaurus was the finest in the ancient world. This amazing structure built in the third century B.C. seated 14,000 people. Each one was able to hear the dialogue perfectly.

Even today, visitors love to try the famous acoustics experiment. They speak softly from any point on the stage, and someone in the highest row of seats can hear them clearly. Today the Epidaurus Festival presents ancient Greek dramas in the theater every weekend from July through September.

Arts and Crafts

The ancient Greek art of pottery is very much alive today. Ceramics artists create their wares in small home studios as well as in large, state-sponsored workshops. Ordinarily, a man forms the object as he spins at a pottery wheel, shaping the wet clay with his hands. After it's fired and hardened in a kiln, a woman paints it with decorative designs.

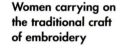

Women carrying on the traditional craft of embroidery

Almost every household in the Greek countryside used to have a weaving loom. Women wove cloth and carpets out of wool, cotton, or silk. Today, Greeks are making a special effort to preserve their weaving traditions. Schools and workshops around the country are producing beautifully designed carpets and textiles. Embroidery is another traditional handicraft, and red is a favorite color.

Regional costumes are brilliant showcases for traditional crafts. Women's costumes are wildly colorful. They're decorated with embroidery, sequins, or jewelry. Men's costumes may feature loose, baggy-sleeved shirts, baggy trousers, high boots, long skirts, or above-the-knee kilts.

Artists to Know

Greece's most famous artist was El Greco ("The Greek"), as he was known in Spain. He was born Domenikos Theotokopoulos in Crete in 1541, and he eventually settled in Toledo, Spain. He's best known for painting religious subjects. His figures have long bodies that look stretched from top to bottom, and the skies in his paintings have an eerie glow.

Nikos Kazantzakis is Greece's best-known modern writer. Born in Crete, he glorifies the hearty, heroic nature of Cretans. "There is a kind of flame in Crete," he wrote, "something more powerful than either life or death." His novels *Zorba the Greek* and *The Last Temptation of Christ* were made into movies. *The Last Temptation* portrayed Christ as much more human than godlike. It was so shocking to the Greek Orthodox Church that it expelled the author from the faith.

Moviegoers fell in love with actress Melina Mercouri when she starred in *Never on Sunday* (1960). When she spoke out against Greece's military dictators, however, the government stripped her of her citizenship. Years later, after democracy was restored, Mercouri served as her country's Minister of Culture.

Melina Mercouri

The National Archaeological Museum

The National Archaeological Museum in Athens is one of the richest archaeological museums in the world. It has artifacts from every culture that flourished in Greece. The gold "Agamemnon mask" from Mycenae is one of its most famous items. It also contains marble statues from the Cycladic period and statues from ancient gravesites, as well as bronze figures of horsemen, warriors, and gods.

Museums for Every Interest

Greece has more archaeological museums than any other country in the world. Many ancient sites have their own museum of excavated treasures. Crete's Herakleion Museum contains almost all the discoveries of the Minoan civilization. Some of the best ancient finds, however, now rest in Athens's National Archaeological Museum.

Dozens of museums throughout the country feature Byzantine art. The Byzantine Museum in Athens displays Byzantine icons, illuminated manuscripts, and ceremonial objects encrusted with precious stones. Many monasteries, too, have their own museums of Byzantine-era treasures.

Athens's Museum of Greek Folk Art is just one of the many centers devoted to Greek folklore and folk art. Other museums cover natural history, science and technology, music, theater, cinema, and seafaring culture.

The Olympics—Back Home Again

Greeks didn't exactly invent sports. However, the world's most famous sports event has its roots in ancient Greece. Olympia was the site of the first Olympic Games in 776 B.C. With only a few exceptions, they took place every four years for the next 1,170 years.

Fifteen hundred years after the ancient games died, the Olympics were born again—in Greece. A Frenchman, Baron Pierre de Coubertin, hounded authorities until they revived the games. The first modern Olympic Games took place in Athens's stadium in 1896. Only 13 countries and 311 athletes took part.

Konstan the Fearless

He came out of nowhere, they said. None of the other competitors had even heard of him. But Konstantinos Kenteris won Olympic gold in the men's 200-meter race in the 2000 Olympics in Sydney, Australia. Konstantinos was the first Greek runner to take a gold medal since the first modern Olympic Games in Athens in 1896. Before his victory, the twenty-seven-year-old sprinter spent several years in Greece training and taking care of injuries.

"I didn't come here to lose," he said in Sydney. "I came here to win. I said Konstan the Greek would win. I feared nobody."

The year 2000 was a great one for Greek athletes. Greek sprinters, gymnasts, discus throwers, and weightlifters took home thirteen medals from the Olympics, which were held

Worth His Weight in Gold

Before Pyrros Dimas won the gold for weightlifting at Barcelona, Spain, in 1992, Greece had won only two Olympic gold medals since 1896. Back home, Greeks

showered Dimas with rose petals and laurels. In 1996, he broke his own world record to win the gold again in Atlanta, Georgia. His gold medal in the 2000 Sydney games in Australia made him only the second weightlifter in Olympic history to win gold in three consecutive Olympics. Born in northern Epirus in 1971, Dimas competes in the 159-pound (72-kg) category. He's physically strong, but even his opponents admire his psychological strength. "He never freezes mentally," one said. Dimas takes a humble attitude: "My own worst enemy is myself, not other athletes."

in Sydney, Australia. For Greek sports fans, more good news was afoot. The games would return to the land of their birth for the 2004 Summer Olympic Games in Athens.

Spectator Sports

Football—what Americans call soccer—is the national sport. Greeks are fiercely loyal to their favorite local, regional, and national soccer clubs. Fans packed the stands in the summer of 2001 when Athens hosted qualifying matches for the 2002 soccer World Cup.

Greece is a popular venue for international sports championships. It's been the scene of the World Greco-Roman Wrestling Championship, the World Weightlifting Championship, the volleyball and basketball world championships, and many more.

Important sports events are held in the Olympic Sports Center, northeast of Athens's city center, and the Peace and Friendship Stadium in Piraeus.

Outdoor Recreation

Sunny Greece lures people from all over the world to its beaches and seaside resorts. With thousands of miles of coastline, Greece offers plenty of sandy beaches for sunbathing. Windsurfing is the most popular water sport. Other favorites are swimming, sailing, and water skiing. Snorkeling is widely popular, but scuba diving is forbidden by law. The law is meant to keep people from stealing underwater archaeological treasures.

Mountains cover two-thirds of Greece, and snow skiers make the most of the slopes. The ski season runs from

Hiking on Amorgos

December through March, but skiing can last into May on the higher peaks. Greece has about two dozen ski resorts. Arachova, near Delphi on Mount Parnassus, is the largest, and it draws the biggest crowds. Bumper-to-bumper traffic inches through its narrow streets on winter weekends.

It's easy to go hiking in Greece. Donkeys and goats have already worn paths through the countryside. Hikers enjoy the hilly Peloponnese, the forested Pindus Range, and southwestern Crete. The six-hour hike through Crete's Samarian Gorge is a breathtaking experience. Serious trekkers take Greece's section of the European Long-Distance Footpath, between Macedonia and the Peloponnese. The toughest part is the route up Mount Parnassus to Delphi. Greeks enjoy mountain biking and rock climbing, too.

Slices of Life

Women family members gather for a visit.

City life and life in the countryside are two different worlds in Greece, but they share a common bond— the family. Family ties have always been an important part of Greek society. Most businesses in Greece are small, family-owned operations. Family ties permeate the big industries, too. Much of Greece's shipping industry, for example, is in the hands of a few wealthy extended families.

Greek families are tight-knit, and family members take care of one another. The family is always available to support someone who is having a hard time. Even though many people are unemployed, they don't live in the streets but at home. Retirement homes are rare in Greece, too. Grandparents usually live with their children's families until they die.

Opposite: **Grandfather and grandsons sharing quality time**

Greek National Holidays

New Year's Day	January 1
Epiphany	January 6
Clean Monday (beginning of Lent)	date varies
Greek Independence Day	March 25
Greek Orthodox Easter	Good Friday through Easter Monday
May Day or Labor Day	May 1
Whit Monday	Day after Pentecost
Dormition (Assumption) of the Virgin Mary	August 15
Ochi Day	October 28
Christmas	December 25 and 26

Greeks today tend to have small families because of financial concerns. They want to be able to give their children all they need. Rural villagers may have three or four children, while city dwellers may have just one or two, because city living is so expensive.

Most young people live with their families until they marry. Even if they leave home for the city, they keep strong ties with their families and rural communities. They're likely to head back to their rural homes for feasts and holidays, and many own land near their rural relatives' homes.

City Life

Big-city life in Greece is crowded and hectic, just as it is in any other European city. Shops, markets, and high-rise apartments and office buildings line the streets. Athens's population has so outgrown its space that congested traffic and air pollution are constant problems.

It's everyone's dream to own a home, but about half the people in Greece's cities live in rented apartments. Middle-class Athenians live in the city, while wealthier people live outside the city center. Families with a comfortable income often keep a second home for summers and holidays.

Most Greek cities have an old section containing narrow cobblestone streets lined with shops, markets, taverns, and cafés.

Narrow street in the Plaka, the old section of Athens

In good weather, people enjoy eating and drinking in the fresh air. The Plaka district, at the foot of the Acropolis, is Athens's old town. Although it's usually jammed with tourists, it's still a pleasant and picturesque nook within the bustling city.

City nights are late nights. Dinner is rarely served before 9:00 or 10:00, and many people eat after 11:00. Then they meet with friends and go to music shows, bars, or discos until the wee hours.

Rural Life—A Slower Pace

Life is much slower and quieter in the countryside than in cities. Many homes are built of stucco and have red tile roofs. In the yards you may see flower and vegetable gardens, a chicken pen, a donkey, and a couple of goats. Since the 1960s, however, more and more people have abandoned their farms or flocks to work in the cities.

Social life goes on outdoors in the hot summer months. Once the blazing sun sets, people enjoy strolling up and down the main streets or along the seaside. Cafés and coffeehouses are popular all year 'round.

Men gathered at a coffeehouse in Crete

Warding Off Evil

You see it on doors, windowsills, furniture, and church domes in Greece—a shocking turquoise blue that seems to leap out from the whitewashed walls. This color is like a trademark throughout the Cyclades Islands. It is used because of an ancient belief that this shade of blue keeps evil away—that bad spirits cannot get past it. Ancient Greeks made the pigment from powdered turquoise or lapis lazuli stones or from the indigo plant. They called the color *kyanos*, from which we get the words cyan (printer's blue) and cyanide.

Lounging around the *kafenion*, or Greek coffeehouse, is a long-standing village tradition. The kafenion used to be strictly male territory. Men would gather there for hours to talk about work, politics, the latest news, and the changing society. A pack of cards or a *tavli* (backgammon) game was standard equipment.

Now, both men and women might be seen in a kafenion, although old men are still the major patrons. Young people tend to seek out trendier places for socializing. Television and other entertainments are replacing traditional social customs.

Spanakópita (Spinach Pie)

Ingredients:

1 10-oz. package of frozen spinach, thawed

1 24-oz. container of cottage cheese

4 eggs

1 tablespoon salt

1 tablespoon flour

1/4 pound feta cheese

1 package filo (phyllo) dough

Cooking oil or butter

Directions:

Preheat the oven to 350°F. In a large bowl, combine the spinach, cottage cheese, eggs, salt, flour, and feta cheese. Mix well. Grease a baking pan with oil. Lay about half the filo dough on the bottom of the pan and brush it with oil or butter. Spread the mixed ingredients evenly across the dough. Lay the other half of the filo dough on top and brush it with oil or butter. Bake for 30 to 40 minutes. Cut into rectangles to serve.

Eating, Greek Style

Meals in Greece are simple but delicious. They're a bountiful mix of fresh foods straight from the farm—tomatoes, onions, garlic, olives, olive oil, fruit, goat cheese, yogurt, and fresh-baked bread.

Lamb is the most common meat, but chicken, beef, pork, and seafood are also available fresh. Swordfish, red mullet, sole, mackerel, and sardines are plentiful, and so are octopus (*oktapódia*), kalamári, shrimp, and mussels. *Taramosaláta* is a pinkish-orange purée of fish eggs.

Feta, the national cheese, is made from goats' milk. Crumbly, white, and salty, it's an essential ingredient in salads.

Traditional Greek salads contain no lettuce. Instead, they're made of tomatoes, cucumbers, onions, feta, and olives.

Typical Greek bread comes in big, round loaves. *Pita* is a round flatbread. With a helping of meat and vegetables in the center, it can be rolled up to make a tube-shaped sandwich. If it's sliced in half, each half can be a pocket for sandwich fillings.

Souvláki sandwiches are as popular and convenient in Greece as hamburgers are in the United States. At souvláki shops, a piece of meat rotates vertically on a rotisserie. The cook slices off strips of meat into a pita and adds tomatoes, onions, and *tzatzíki*, a yogurt sauce with cucumbers and garlic. Souvláki is sometimes served as a kebab—chunks of meat, tomatoes, and onions on a skewer. *Moussaká* is ground meat, eggplant, potatoes, and onions baked with a creamy sauce. *Pastítsio* is layered noodles, meat, and tomato sauce.

Assorted traditional Greek dishes

Breakfast is simple. It may consist only of strong coffee, with perhaps a sesame-seed bagel (*kolouri*) or cheese pie (*tirópita*). Lunch, too, is light, and people often stop by cafés or street stalls for lunchtime snacks. They might order cheese pie, spinach pie (*spanakópita*), fried cheese (*saganáki*), a souvláki sandwich, or grape leaves stuffed with rice and onions (*dolmádes*).

The late evening meal is the high point of the day. For those eating out in a taverna, dinner is served at big tables where diners help themselves to huge platters of food. For Sunday dinners at home, a traditional dish is marinated beef filet. It's usually served with rice that is spiced up with raisins, apricots, or cherries.

Dessert is often fresh fruit—strawberries, watermelon, oranges, grapes, cherries, peaches, or figs. Cakes and pastries are typically served dripping with honey syrup. *Baclavá* is a flaky pastry with walnuts or almonds and cinnamon. *Kadaïfi* are threadlike pastry rolls filled with nuts.

Greek coffee is served in tiny cups. It's thick, strong, and richly flavored. The coffee grounds sink to the bottom of the cup and a creamy foam rests on top. Coffee drinkers have three choices: very sweet (*gliko*), slightly sweet (*metrio*), or unsweetened (*sketo*).

Namedays and Names

In Greece, people celebrate their nameday, not their birthday. The nameday is the feast of the saint after whom a person is named. It's customary to throw a party, have an open house with a buffet feast, or at least pass out sweets on your nameday.

Naming a child is not a frivolous matter. Children are usually named after saints. A child is never named after a parent, but is often named for a grandparent. The patron saint of the child's city or region is a popular choice, too. When a baby is eight days old, it receives its name in a special Greek Orthodox service. In a nonreligious family, parents may choose a name with ancient significance, such as Aristotle or Aphrodite.

Holidays and Festivals

A candlelit procession

Any time of year is likely to be festival time in some part of Greece. Saints' days abound, and every town and village celebrates its favorite patron saints. Most festivals in Greece are Christian, while some have their roots in ancient lore.

Carnival season—*Apokries*—usually begins in February. It lasts for three weeks before the pre-Easter Lenten season begins. People dress in fancy costumes and eat, drink, and dance. The most spectacular festivities take place in Patras and in Athens's Plaka.

The Easter season is the most important religious festival of the year, with candlelit processions, fireworks, and lavish meals. On Good Friday, people carry candles through the streets in the *Epitaphios*, a funeral procession for Christ.

Holy Saturday fireworks

Holy Saturday night finds the faithful gathered in church for the Easter Vigil. When the priest announces that Christ is risen, people light candles from one to the other with fire from the Easter candle. Church bells ring and fireworks explode into the night sky. In many villages, a huge bonfire consumes an image of Judas the traitor. Back at home, people eat *majiritsa* soup to break their pre-Easter fast. It's a traditional soup made with lamb, egg, lemon juice, and plenty of dill.

On Easter Sunday, people feast on lamb roasted on a spit. Keeping up a folk tradition, each person takes a red-dyed Easter egg and knocks it against others' eggs. The person whose egg doesn't crack is thought to have good luck for a whole year.

August 15 is the second-biggest religious holiday. It's the feast of the Dormition, known elsewhere as the Assumption of the Virgin Mary. On the island of Tinos, thousands of pilgrims converge on the Church of St. Mary. Its icon is believed to have miraculous powers.

On Christmas Eve, children go from house to house caroling and collecting treats. People in the countryside keep up old traditions such as singing, dancing, and roasting a pig. In the cities, however, most people put up a Christmas tree in their homes and decorate it with festive ornaments. Only children receive gifts, however.

New Year's Day in Greece is also the feast of St. Basil. In Byzantine tradition, a coin is baked into the *Vasilopitta* (Basil cake). Tradition says that whoever gets the slice with the coin shall enjoy a year of good luck. St. Basil's Day, rather than Christmas, is the day for gift-giving among family and friends.

Epiphany, January 6, brings the Christmas season to a close. It's the day for the Blessing of the Waters. In Pireaus and other port cities, a priest blesses small boats and ships. For the main event of the day, he blesses a cross and throws it into the sea. Then, daring young men plunge into the icy waters and swim after it. Whoever finds the cross, it is said, will be blessed with—what else?—good luck throughout the year to come!

Women Rule!

Villagers in some Thracian towns switch roles for the *Gynaikokratia* holiday (January 8). *Gynaikokratia* was the name of an ancient Greek comedy, and the word means "Women Rule." This is the day when women of the village hang out in cafés where men usually gather, while the men stay home cooking, cleaning house, and taking care of children. At nightfall, the men join the women for a celebration.

Timeline

Greek History

The Hellenic civilization flourishes on what is now known as Greece.	3000 B.C.
Mycenae falls.	1200 B.C.
First Olympic games are held.	776 B.C.
Golden Age of Greece flourishes under the rule of Pericles.	461–429 B.C.
Constantine makes Byzantium (renamed Constantinople) the capital of the Roman Empire.	A.D. 330
The Byzantine Empire, including Greece, falls to the Ottoman Empire.	1453

World History

2500 B.C.	Egyptians build the Pyramids and the Sphinx in Giza.
563 B.C.	The Buddha is born in India.
A.D. 313	The Roman emperor Constantine recognizes Christianity.
610	The Prophet Muhammad begins preaching a new religion called Islam.
1054	The Eastern (Orthodox) and Western (Roman) Churches break apart.
1066	William the Conqueror defeats the English in the Battle of Hastings.
1095	Pope Urban II proclaims the First Crusade.
1215	King John seals the Magna Carta.
1300s	The Renaissance begins in Italy.
1347	The Black Death sweeps through Europe.
1492	Columbus arrives in North America.
1500s	The Reformation leads to the birth of Protestantism.
1776	The Declaration of Independence is signed.

Greek History

The Greek war of independence against the Ottomans begins.	1821
Ioannis Kapodistrias becomes the first prime minister of Greece.	1827
Greece gains independence from the Ottomans.	1829
Heinrich Schliemann excavates the ancient city of Troy.	1868
First Olympic Games of the modern era are held in Athens.	1896
Greece says "No!" to Mussolini.	1940
Army officers seize the Greek government in a military coup.	1967
Democracy is restored; Greece is proclaimed a republic.	1973
Andreas Papandreou forms Greece's first socialist government; Greece joins the European Union.	1981
Summer Olympics return to Athens.	2004

World History

1789	The French Revolution begins.
1865	The American Civil War ends.
1914	World War I breaks out.
1917	The Bolshevik Revolution brings communism to Russia.
1929	Worldwide economic depression begins.
1939	World War II begins, following the German invasion of Poland.
1945	World War II ends.
1957	The Vietnam War starts.
1969	Humans land on the moon.
1975	The Vietnam War ends.
1979	Soviet Union invades Afghanistan.
1983	Drought and famine in Africa.
1989	The Berlin Wall is torn down, as communism crumbles in Eastern Europe.
1991	Soviet Union breaks into separate states.
1992	Bill Clinton is elected U.S. president.
2000	George W. Bush is elected U.S. president.

Fast Facts

Official name:	Hellenic Republic
Capital:	Athens
Official language:	Greek

Athens

Greece's flag

Mount Olympus

Religion:	Greek Orthodox (98% of citizens)
Independence:	1829
National anthem:	"Hymn to Freedom," adopted in 1864 Words by Dionysos Solomós (1798–1857), music by Nikolaos Mantzaros (1795–1873)
Government:	Parliamentary republic
Head of state:	President
Head of government:	Prime minister
Area:	50,942 square miles (131,940 sq km)
Highest elevation:	Mount Olympus, 9,570 feet (2,917 m)
Lowest elevation:	Sea level along the Mediterranean Sea
Number of islands:	More than 2,000; 170 populated
Largest island:	Crete, 3,189 square miles (8,260 sq km)
Average annual precipitation:	51 inches (128 cm) in Corfu; 16 inches (40 cm) in Athens
Length of coastline:	9,333 miles (15,020 km)
Greatest distance, north-south:	350 miles (587 km)
Greatest distance, east-west:	345 miles (555 km)
Main rivers:	Alfios, Eurotas, Nestos, Pinios
Main lakes:	Lake Vistonis, Lake Volviis
Major bodies of water:	Aegean Sea, Sea of Crete, Ionian Sea, Mediterranean Sea

Ruins of Palace of Minos

Highest recorded temperatures:	Athens: 108°F (42°C); Thessaloniki 108°F (42°C)
Lowest recorded temperatures:	Athens: 25°F (-3°C); Thessaloniki 14° F (-10°C)
National population (2001 census):	10,939,771

Population of largest cities:

Athens (city only)	772,072
Thessaloniki (city only)	383,967
Piraeus	182,671
Patras	153,344
Herakleion	116,178

Famous landmarks:
- ▶ ***Parthenon, on the Acropolis***, Athens
- ▶ ***Ancient Agora***, Athens
- ▶ ***Ruins at Delphi, Olympia, Corinth, Troy, and Mycenae***
- ▶ ***Palace of Knossos***, Crete

Industry: Services are Greece's largest industry. They include education, health care, banking, government work, and tourism. Leading manufactured goods include food products, chemicals, metal items, and clothing. Leading farm products are wheat, corn, olives, sugar beets, and sheep.

Currency: Through 2001: the drachma
Beginning in 2002: the Euro

System of weights and measures: Metric

Literacy (1990 est.): 95%

The drachma, Greece's currency before the introduction of the Euro in 2002.

Children in costume

Maria Callas

Common Greek words and phrases:

kaliméra (kah-lee-MEH-rah)	good day
kalispéra (kah-lee-SPEH-rah)	good evening
kaliníkhta (kah-lee-NEEK-tah)	good night
ne (neh)	yes
ochi (OH-shee)	no
parakaló (pah-rah-kah-LOH)	please
efkharistó (ef-kah-rees-TOH)	thank you
ti kanis? (tee KAH-nees)	how are you?

Famous Greek:

Aristotle   (384–322 B.C.)
Philosopher

Maria Callas   (1923–1977)
Opera singer

Euclid   (365–300 B.C.)
Mathematician known as the "father of geometry"

Hippocrates   (460?–370? B.C.)
First doctor to use scientific methods

Ioannis Kapodistrias   (1776–1831)
Political leader; first prime minister

Nikos Kazantzakis   (1885–1957)
Novelist

Aristotle Onassis   (1906–1975)
Shipping magnate

Plato   (427–347 B.C.)
Philosopher

Pythagoras   (570–496 B.C.)
Mathematician

Socrates   (470–399 B.C.)
Philosopher

Mikis Theodorakis   (1925–)
Composer

Domenikos Theotokopoulos ("El Greco")   (1541–1614)
Artist

To Find Out More

Nonfiction

▶ Blyton, Enid. *Tales of Ancient Greece*. London: HarperCollins UK, 1998.

▶ Connolly, Peter. *The Ancient City: Life in Classical Athens and Rome*. New York: Oxford University Press, 2000.

▶ Dubois, Jill. *Greece* (Cultures of the World). Tarrytown, NY: Benchmark Books, 1995.

▶ Ferris, Julie, and Julie Guerrero. *Ancient Greece: A Guide to the Golden Age of Greece*. New York: Larousse Kingfisher Chambers, 1999.

▶ Miles, Lisa, and Jane Chisholm. *Encyclopedia of Ancient Greece*. San Jose: EDC Publications, 2000.

▶ Nardo, Don. *Greece* (Modern Nations of the World). Farmington Hills, MI: Lucent Books, 2000.

▶ Pearson, Anne. *Eyewitness: Ancient Greece*. London: DK Publishing, 2000.

▶ Stein, R. Conrad. *Athens* (Cities of the World). Danbury, CT: Children's Press, 1997.

▶ Tames, Richard. *Step into Ancient Greece*. London: Lorenz Books, 1999.

Videotapes

▶ *Art of the Western World. Set 1: Greece*. 50 minutes. Social Studies School Service, 1989.

▶ *Athenian Democracy*. 15 minutes. Encyclopaedia Britannica, 1993.

▶ *Athens and Ancient Greece: Great Cities of the Ancient World*. 78 minutes. Social Studies School Service, 1994.

▶ *Greece: Athens, the Peloponnese, and the Greek Islands*. 52 minutes. Travel Video Cyberstore, 1999.

▶ *Myths and Legends of Ancient Greece*. 20 minutes. Rainbow Educational Video, 1995.

Web Sites

▶ **The Greeks: Crucible of Civilization**
http://www.pbs.org/empires/thegreeks/
An interactive exploration of Greek culture, civilization, and daily life.

▶ **The Embassy of Greece**
http://www.greekembassy.org
Information on Greek people, history, geography, culture, economy, archaeological sites, and more.

▶ **Ancient Greece**
http://www.ancientgreece.com
An in-depth survey of the history, mythology, people, wars, and art of ancient Greece.

▶ **The Cradle of Western Civilization**
http://mrdowling.com/701greece.html
Fascinating information on Greek mythology, Homer, Socrates, Plato, Alexander the Great, and other great people of ancient Greece.

Embassy

▶ **Embassy of Greece**
2221 Massachusetts Ave., NW
Washington, DC 20008
(202) 939-5800

Index

Page numbers in *italics* indicate illustrations.

Meet the Author

ANN HEINRICHS fell in love with faraway places while reading Doctor Dolittle books as a child. Now she tries to cover as much of the earth as possible. She has traveled through most of the United States and much of Europe, as well as the Middle East, East Asia, and Africa. In Greece, she enjoyed exploring archaeological sites, trekking through the countryside, scrambling across the islands, and devouring Greek food.

Ann grew up roaming the woods of Arkansas. Now she lives in Chicago. She is the author of more than seventy books for children and young adults on American, European, Asian, and African history and culture. Several of her books have won national and state awards.

"To me, writing nonfiction is a bigger challenge than writing fiction. With nonfiction, you can't just dream something up—everything has to be true. Finding out facts is harder than making things up, but to me it's more rewarding. When I uncover the facts, they always turn out to be more spectacular than fiction could ever be. And I'm always on the lookout for what kids in another country are up to, so I can report back to kids here."

Ann has also written numerous newspaper, magazine, and encyclopedia articles. As an advertising copywriter, she has covered every subject from plumbing hardware to Oriental rugs. She holds bachelor's and master's degrees in piano performance. But these days, her performing arts are t'ai chi empty-hand and sword forms. She is an award-winning martial artist and participates in regional and national tournaments.

Photo Credits

A Perfect Exposure: 16, 22, 77, 115 (Anavasi), 31, 32, 89 top (Marios Fournaris), 72, 73, 86, 93, 119 (Vassilis Sarioglou), 13, 19, 20 right, 23 top, 85 (Thanasis Stavrakis), 2, 120 (Yannis Vlamos)

AllSport USA/Getty Images/Rick Stewart: 113 bottom

Ann Heinrichs: 28 top, 78, 80 bottom

Art Resource, NY: 42 bottom (Giraudon/ Museo Archaeologico, Taranto, Italy) 25, 36 (Erich Lessing), 44 top (Erich Lessing/Archaeological Museum, Istanbul, Turkey), 48 (Erich Lessing/ Cathedral, Cologne, Germany), 34 (Nimatallah/National Archaeological Museum, Athens, Greece), 51 (Victoria & Albert Museum, London)

Bridgeman Art Library International Ltd., London/New York: 55 (Marine College, St. Petersburg, Russia), 35, 132 top (Ali Meyer), 43 (Museo d'Arte Moderno di Ca Pesaro, Venice, Italy)

Corbis Images: 84 top (Yann Arthus-Bertrand), 109, 111, 133 bottom (Bettman), 59 (Hulton-Deutsch Collection), 12, 133 top (Daniel Laine), 91 (Richard List), 106, 107 (Gail Mooney), 69 (Vittoriano Rastelli), 99, 105, 113 top (Reuters NewMedia Inc.), 70 (David Rubinger)

MapQuest.com, Inc.: 64, 131 top

Mark J. Burdolski: 143

Mary Evans Picture Library: 40 (Edwin Wallace), 37, 38 top, 39, 41, 42 top, 47 top, 47 bottom, 49, 57 bottom, 57 top

On Location: 84 bottom, 87, 88 (V. Constantineas), 17 right, 20 left, 33, 54, 61, 79, 126, 131 bottom (Loukas Hapsis), 108 (Maro Kouri), 10 top, 28 bottom, 30 bottom (Thanos Labropoulos), 10 bottom, 26, 29 bottom, 96, 97 (Roberto Meazza), 18, 75, 76, 102, 116, 123, 132 bottom (Clairy Moustafellou), 30 top (Costas Picadas), 7 bottom, 17 left, 45 bottom, 63 bottom (Massimo Pizzocaro) 29 top (Alex Rodopoulos), 82, 95 (Aris Vafeiadakis), 23 bottom, 24 bottom, 89 bottom, 101, 110, 117, 125 (Velissarios Voutsas)

Stone/Getty Images: 14 (Robert Everts), 24 top (George Grigoriou), 60 (David Hanson), 80 top (Will & Deni McIntyre), 63 top, 130 left (Donald Nausbaum), 8, 121 (Hugh Sitton), 7 top, 104 (Hans Strand), cover, back cover, 6, 27 (Charlie Waite)

Maps by Joe LeMonnier